Why Don't Psychotherap Laugh?

The capacity for humour is one of life's blessings. So why is it so lacking in the theory and even the practice of analysis and therapy? This is the first book of its kind about a neglected and even taboo topic: the place of enjoyment and good humour in psychotherapy.

Why Don't Psychotherapists Laugh? traces the development of professional psychotherapy and its almost exclusive focus on life's tragedies. This may naturally suit some practitioners; others may learn that a proper therapeutic persona is serious, even solemn. But what are they and their clients missing? Ann Shearer draws on ideas about humour and its functions from antiquity to contemporary stand-up comedy and beyond, to explore how it works in both mind and body. She shows how even the blackest humour may yield psychological information, and how humour can help build therapeutic relationships and be a catalyst for healing. Through real-life stories from consulting rooms, told by both therapists and clients, the author shows how a sense of enjoyment and good humour can restore life to people in distress – and how destructive a lack of these may become.

This book provides a resource for further reflection on the therapeutic task. It will also intrigue anyone who wants to know more about the kinds of people psychotherapists are, what they do and why. Written in a highly accessible style, *Why Don't Psychotherapists Laugh?* will appeal to psychotherapists with a range of training and allegiances, their teachers in vocational and academic institutions and their clients, as well as to readers with an interest in psychotherapy, humour and psychology.

Ann Shearer is a Jungian analyst based in London. She lectures internationally and for two years was a Royal Literary Fund Writing Fellow at Imperial College London. Previously a journalist and consultant in social welfare, her many articles and ten books include (with Pamela Donleavy) *From Ancient Myth to Modern Healing: Themis: goddess of heart-soul, justice and reconciliation* (Routledge, 2008).

Why Don't Psychotherapists Laugh?

Enjoyment and the consulting room

Ann Shearer

Routledge
Taylor & Francis Group
LONDON AND NEW YORK

First published 2016
by Routledge
2 Park Square, Milton Park, Abingdon, Oxon OX14 4RN

and by Routledge
711 Third Avenue, New York, NY 10017

Routledge is an imprint of the Taylor & Francis Group, an informa business

© 2016 Ann Shearer

The right of Ann Shearer to be identified as author of this work has been asserted by her in accordance with sections 77 and 78 of the Copyright, Designs and Patents Act 1988.

All rights reserved. No part of this book may be reprinted or reproduced or utilised in any form or by any electronic, mechanical, or other means, now known or hereafter invented, including photocopying and recording, or in any information storage or retrieval system, without permission in writing from the publishers.

Trademark notice: Product or corporate names may be trademarks or registered trademarks, and are used only for identification and explanation without intent to infringe.

British Library Cataloguing in Publication Data
A catalogue record for this book is available from the British Library

Library of Congress Cataloging in Publication Data
Names: Shearer, Ann, 1943– author.
Title: Why don't psychotherapists laugh? : enjoyment and the consulting room / Ann Shearer.
Description: Abingdon, Oxon ; New York, NY : Routledge, 2016. | Includes bibliographical references.
Identifiers: LCCN 2015039744| ISBN 9781138899605 (hardback) | ISBN 9781138899612 (pbk.)
Subjects: LCSH: Laughter–Psychological aspects. | Psychotherapy. | Psychotherapists.
Classification: LCC BF575.L3 S44 2016 | DDC 616.89/14–dc23
LC record available at http://lccn.loc.gov/2015039744

ISBN: 978-1-138-89960-5 (hbk)
ISBN: 978-1-138-89961-2 (pbk)
ISBN: 978-1-315-70773-0 (ebk)

Typeset in Times New Roman
by Wearset Ltd, Boldon, Tyne and Wear
Printed by Ashford Colour Press Ltd.

MIX
Paper from responsible sources
FSC® C011748

Contents

Acknowledgements — vii

1 Starting points — 1
2 A goddess laughs — 11

Humour and the healers — 17

3 In theory — 19
4 Looking outwards — 29
5 Looking inwards — 39

What's so funny? — 49

6 Senses of humour — 51
7 Shadow stories — 61
8 Bodies and brains — 69

In the consulting room — 79

9 Thresholds — 81
10 Power and promise — 89

11 Bridges and boundaries	99
12 No laughing matter?	109
13 Stories of life and death	117
14 Looking back	127
Bibliography	131
Index	139

Acknowledgements

As a wise old friend used to say, 'We all shout loudest about our own weakest points'. Ever since my childhood, people have told me that I'm 'too serious'. So thanks go first to all those many friends, colleagues, patients and clients who have taught me so much over the years about how to lighten up and see the world through a more humorous lens. A particular mention goes to the Association of Independent Psychotherapists in London, who many years ago set me thinking when they invited me to talk at their conference on 'Uses and Abuses of Humour in Psychotherapy'.

None of my patients appears in these pages. But other people's do, and I'm grateful to Jane Haynes, Stephen Grosz, Donald Kalsched and Irvin Yalom for their generous response to the use I've made of their therapeutic stories. Between them, they draw on the relational, psychoanalytic, Jungian and existential traditions. This was not deliberate on my part, but it's a happy illustration that appreciation of the humorous is far from being the preserve of any one therapeutic approach.

Acknowledgements are also due to:

Bill Hamilton as the Literary Executor of the Estate of the Late Sonia Brownell Orwell for permission to quote from *Nineteen Eighty-Four* by George Orwell (Copyright © George Orwell, 1949).

The Provost and Scholars of King's College, Cambridge and the Society of Authors as the Literary Representative of the Estate of E.M. Forster for permission to quote from *Howard's End.*

Random House, W.W. Norton, Perseus Books and the Marsh Agency Ltd on behalf of Sigmund Freud Copyrights for permission to quote from *The Standard Edition of the Complete Psychological Works of Sigmund Freud.*

Taylor & Francis and Princeton University Press for permission to quote from *The Collected Works of C.G. Jung.*

Full details of these publications are in the Bibliography.

Chapter 1

Starting points

Looking back over more than two decades as a Jungian analyst, I count myself fortunate. I think of all I've learned about the extraordinary, even awe-inspiring endurance of the human spirit, of the infinitely subtle ways of psyche in its quest for self-fulfilment, of the variety of people in whose stories I've been privileged to participate, of friends and colleagues in many parts of the world and of abiding intellectual stimulation. As in life itself, there have been times of boredom, irritation, anger and grief. But these have been hugely outweighed by the interest, affection and flashes of shared delight. Overall though, one thing seems to have been in short supply: an enjoyment, even celebration, of what makes life a humorous business as well as a testing and sometimes tragic one. This quality is not easy to define – not least because each person will find it in their own way. But we recognise it when it comes to us, when we smile or laugh or even guffaw. And we know the dull heaviness that can weigh on us when it's not there. In this book, I call it 'humour' – a catchall for that sense of the humorous which enables us to live more good-humouredly with what life may bring, and so be more open to its joys as well as its sorrows.

That this quality has been neglected in discussions within and about psychotherapy seems peculiar, when we consider that the rest of the world has known since time immemorial about humour's power to heal the suffering mind and heart. The colleagues I know best have been other analysts and depth psychologists who at least (and sometimes at most) share a perception that the conscious world of rational mind is underpinned and often subverted by something we call 'the unconscious'. Within that spectrum, I count myself a fairly classical Jungian. That must inevitably inform my perceptions, but I have travelled more widely too and found the same: psychotherapy and humour just don't seem easy together. The literature seems to bear this out: I've been quite surprised to discover how seldom humour gets even a mention in professional textbooks. This book is about why this might be so, and what psychotherapists, those who consult them and indeed others might be missing.

Whatever may be going on in the confidentiality of the consulting room, something seems to happen once we therapists appear in public, once we present a professional persona to the wider world and even to each other. I think of professional gatherings of reverent heaviness, the downward shift in the speaker's voice and demeanour as they set their face to serious, rustle their papers and read their lecture in tones of a deliberate gravity. I think of drowsing over books and journals, weighed down by their tone, wondering how an occupation so potentially enlivening can get to sound so ponderous. Of course psychotherapy is a serious business. The therapy of psyche, the witnessing of the soul's stirrings as someone becomes more attuned to their own complexity, better able both to accept their limitation and darkness and to rejoice in a wider sense of meaning in their life: there is nothing in the least unserious in that, for the individual, those around them and even, as Jung believed and I hope, for the collective consciousness of our time. But do we have to be *solemn* about it?

The gravity of psychotherapy's persona may weigh particularly heavy at the analytic end of the spectrum. But it's by no means restricted to it. In Britain at least, the rigours of psychoanalytic technique seem to have cast a miasma over 'psychodynamic' consulting rooms and counselling ones as well. My friend Elizabeth Wilde McCormick recalls the delighted relief with which her students of transpersonal psychology greeted her clinical seminar on 'Are we allowed to laugh?' Already they, who might be thought immune from the miasma, had somehow picked up the idea that laughter might not be part of responsible practice. Perhaps they felt that it would be an insult to the pain and distress that impels people to seek therapy, or simply confirm their clients' fears that they will not be taken seriously, even laughed at behind their back. Yet, as I hope will become clear through these chapters, the raw material of psychological distress is precisely what humour may help to heal. People who entrust themselves to psychotherapy may both lack and need its blessings.

Academic writers about humour like to talk about *gelasts* and *agelasts*; their concern is with the *gelastic* mode. All these derive from the Greek meaning 'laughter': those who laugh, those who don't and what makes for the difference between them. But it's tempting to play with the sounds to hear as well something about 'elasticity', even the wobbly jelly which still manages to keep its essential shape. This is what humour can do for us. It can bring a greater flexibility to over-rigid and one-sided attitudes; it can expand our self-awareness and help bridge the discrepancy between conscious and unconscious tendencies in which neurosis thrives. Humour can bring much-needed perspective. One of the unbearable aspects of depression is that in its blackness there is no sense that the world could be different. One of the curses of a malign perception of personal 'specialness' – of being either superior or inferior to everyone else – is that it cloaks such a terrible sense of isolation from the rest of the human world. To such states and others too, humour can bring the possibility of relief.

So whether psychotherapists make place for humour, or even encourage it, may matter quite a lot to people who consult them. It may also matter more widely. Especially at the psychoanalytic end, psychotherapy can seem remote indeed from everyday life – a ritual that people 'go to' once a week or more to make them 'feel better'. The more often people attend the ritual, the more obscure it may appear to outsiders, couched now in ideas and language that can seem frankly incomprehensible. This is no new perception. Already in 1955 the American psychoanalyst Robert Lindner, himself a great populariser, was finding that

> around psychoanalysis there has been built a fence of mystery and something resembling awe. Its practitioners, if not yet the objects of veneration and fear, are well on their way to elevation as priests of a certain kind; and the initiates – those who have lain on couches, that is – threaten to become a confraternity of the saved, a latter-day community of saints whose cancelled checks comprise a passport to heavens denied to those less (or more?) fortunate.[1]

Psychotherapists are not perhaps concerned enough about this sort of perception, not interested enough in communicating more widely ideas that people other than themselves might find interesting, even helpful – or in learning from what 'everyone knows'. The idea of their calling as set apart from the world's rough and tumble may even suit them. They tend to be introverted; many of them seem to enjoy spending a lot of time talking to and squabbling with each other about what their work is about and how to do it. But any psychology is inevitably a product of its practitioners and the culture of which they are a part. They need connection with the wider world too, if they are keep attuned to what I take to be a central aim of all this hard work: that people find a greater ability to live with good humour, enjoyment, creativity and kindliness outside the consulting room.

For all the obscurities, psychotherapy and the world are hardly strangers. The ideas of depth psychology have long since found their way into European and North American culture. People may no longer be surprised, though perhaps they may still be discomfited, to think there is 'an unconscious' with which our rational mind is often in painful conflict, or that we all have a shadow side which we would rather project onto others than acknowledge as our own. While Freud's ideas have had a pervasive intellectual afterlife in the arts and academia, Jung's have possibly travelled more quietly and widely, providing both the basis of psychological testing for job suitability and inspiration to poets, dreamers and seekers. So what psychotherapists believe about the human condition matters not just to their patients and clients: it makes its way subtly, even unconsciously, into the wider culture. And there are a great many therapists. Each therapeutic encounter creates another psychological ripple, which stretches from the individual patient or client to their intimates and through them to who knows how far beyond. The world needs more good humour in its relationships, not less: if it is unwelcome in the consulting room then an opportunity to foster it more widely may be lost.

And really, outside the consulting room, doesn't the entire world know that laughter is the best medicine, that a merry heart does us good? The association of humour and healing is age-old. To take just one instance: today's European pantomime routines have been persuasively traced back to the ancient shamanic rituals of death and re-birth, still glimpsed in traditional societies in many parts of the world.[2] These days, ancient truths have scientific backing. Ever since the 1970s, when Norman Cousins laughed his way out of agonising pain and into health with doses of Marx Brothers films, Vitamin C and focus on positive emotions, there's been research into the beneficial effects of humour on body and soul. Laughter exercises heart and lungs, releases pain-killing endorphins, raises mood. Clowns visit sick children; laughter therapists participate in cancer treatment. Humour works in the mind as well. Exploiting as it so often does the incongruities between expectation and actuality, it enables us to negotiate this uncertain world. 'You've got to laugh' we say when we know the alternative is to weep – and so we find the capacity to survive. 'It's being so cheerful as keeps me going' intoned the lugubrious Mrs Mop in *ITMA*, the British radio comedy beamed out in the darkest days of the Second World War, and everybody roared with laughter; the catchphrase continued to raise ironic mirth in my family long after the war was over, and I suspect in many others as well. We know that it doesn't do to take ourselves and our troubles 'too seriously' and that humour offers us that small step back from our situation which restores it and so us to proportion. Humour helps us find companions along life's way. 'GSOH' comes high on the wish-lists in lonely hearts advertisements; humour can bring people together, build a sense of shared humanity that transcends difference.

And the beauty of it is that the capacity for humour seems to be innate, part of our physiological and psychological makeup. It appears to have been present in the earliest human societies, its origins shared with other primates and maybe other mammals too. In classical Jungian terms, it is an archetypal attribute, an inbuilt potential for both instinctual and psychic experience. For the contemporary affective neuroscientist Jaak Panksepp, its origins may lie in what he calls PLAY, one of the seven primary process emotions encoded in the mammalian brain. He sees 'joyful, rough and tumble social interactions' as providing a fundamental substrate for social learning as well as individual epigenetic modifications of higher social brain functions.[3] Humour is embodied. The very word derives from the Latin 'umor', meaning 'liquid' or 'moisture', and medieval psychosomatic medicine was based on finding the right balance of the four 'humours' in the body of each individual. Too much blood made people sanguine and over-excitable, and an excess of phlegm made for sluggishness; too much black bile led to melancholia and depression, while too much of the yellow sort made people choleric and irritable. When the humours were in balance, people became 'good-humoured', in both body and mind. This old work with the flow and counterflow of our fluidities and fixities is also the craft of the alchemists, in which Jung found such a powerful metaphor for the work towards psychological wholeness. In many texts, it was the ceaseless alternations of *solutio et coagulatio*, dissolving and bringing together, that would finally yield the 'uncommon gold' which for Jung was the Self as image of psyche's totality. Working to bring *solutio* to a self-perception that has become too rigid, or *coagulatio* to an ego that does not yet know its own ground, is still an important part of the therapeutic endeavour, whether 'Jungian' or not.

So it's strange that something as fundamental to human nature seems to have been so left out of psychological writings – and hard too to see why something as usefully revelatory of an individual as their sense of humour should not be encouraged in consulting rooms. Perhaps it is, and these are humorous places after all. Perhaps the startling lack of reference to this aspect of the work is simply one more illustration of the gap between theory and what therapists actually do. Perhaps it is simply too hard to write about. Everyone knows that humour finds it hard to travel between cultures and even individuals. A whole cultural story could be told about American 'humor' and British 'humour', and already my perception of the lack of humour in psychotherapy may simply tell you that I don't get it. Jokes are lost in translation, as anyone who has drooped over Freud's *Jokes and Their Relation to the Unconscious* in English could confirm; every comic knows that a joke that needs explaining is a joke that has died. Humour is of the moment. How often does the recounting of an extremely funny experience tail away into a limp 'Well, you had to be there...'? Perhaps this is one reason that there is so little humour in psychotherapeutic case reports: its actions may be too hard to convey with conviction beyond the interactive moment. When that moment is already obscured by the necessary fictionalising of one of the people involved and the habitual reticence of the other, then what chance is there of readers really getting the point?

Yet when I've mentioned the title of this book to colleagues, the range of reactions suggests that something else may also be going on. Some have immediately smiled, or chuckled appreciatively, cheering it on as a topic worth exploring. But others have looked dubious, even bristled. Perhaps they suspect that I am *not properly serious*. Lightness of heart is one of life's great blessings. But 'light-hearted' can too easily be interpreted as 'frivolous'. The comic mode has always been less valued than the tragic; comedy is traditionally seen as lightweight by comparison with tragedy's concern for the great themes of human suffering. There are many valid answers to the title's question. But some colleagues have responded rather crossly, as if they have detected a challenge. 'Well', said one, 'I laugh – *when it's appropriate*' – as if I had suggested something shockingly different. The reaction of other people has been telling too. Most often they have burst out laughing in delighted recognition, though some have seemed somewhat puzzled by the juxtaposition of 'therapy' and 'laughter'. Both these reactions might encourage psychotherapists to wonder about their public image. Importantly, two people thought their own therapist had laughed *too much*: they felt that their troubles were not being taken seriously enough.

Already here's a hint of complexities ahead. Some are built into the project itself. I've been constantly aware of the potential pitfalls of generalising about 'psychotherapists' when individuals and groups among them may follow very different understandings of the human psyche and ways to work with it. I have tried to be even-handed between different approaches, but my swithering between referring to psychotherapists as either 'us' or 'them' will probably tell readers quite a lot about my own sympathies and practice. They will notice too a related indecisiveness about whether to call the people who consult therapists 'patients' or 'clients'. Both terms carry a weight of cultural association. My own preference is for 'patient', not because it makes psychotherapists sound grander, but because it seems more associated with the complexities of healing than the straightforwardness of commercial transaction conjured by 'client'. I like the old associations of 'patient' – one who is capable of suffering, or experiencing, emotions and enduring these through time.

But these are minor difficulties compared to engaging with the complexities of humour itself. When is it (see above) 'appropriate' or 'too much'? How can we ever be sure it stays the first and doesn't burst out into the second? Humour is unpredictable in its very nature, erupting when we least expect it to take us beyond our intended selves. Hyperbole and exaggeration are its idioms; transgressing established boundaries and challenging fixed certainties are what it does. The more we try to think about it, the more it slips our categorising grasp. Humour is a universal, inbuilt human attribute. Yet it travels along so many paths: from ironical lift of an eyebrow to spluttering belly laugh, from the precision of wit to the snorting of an uncontrollable giggle. How do we even tell that it's there? We often assume a connection between humour and laughter – I've done it myself in this book's title. But of course the two may be quite unrelated: there's nothing good-humoured about a 'mirthless laugh'. Joking may be no more sure a guide. As the tortured personal lives of many professional comedians attest, a saving sense of life's humour is not at all the same as an ability to crack or appreciate a joke. And even when we can detect that there's humour about, its intent is notoriously hard to read. It may be gentle and encouraging or mocking and cruel, an expression of empathic communication or a weapon of power. And we may really not know when it's one or the other. The distinction between laughing *with* and laughing *at* depends almost entirely on the perception of the person on the receiving end. As the philosopher Mary Midgely points out, to understand laughter at all depends on grasping the state of mind of the person making these strange grimaces and snorts, and that in turn depends on the recipient being capable of something like it themselves.[4]

So humour can be dangerous, both between individuals and among them. The beginning of 2015 saw an extreme and terrible example of that, when two Islamist gunmen murdered 11 of the staff of *Charlie Hebdo*, a small, stridently secular humorous magazine in Paris; one other person and a policeman also died. In subsequent attacks, five further people died and others were wounded and terrorised. The *Charlie Hebdo* murders ignited a huge, international outcry: the magazine's scurrilous and often scatological cartoons of religious leaders, whether the Prophet Mohamed or the Pope, became emblems of the freedom of expression. 'Je suis Charlie' became a mantra across the world, as cartoonists published in support and people gathered in huge numbers to assert the inalienable right to free speech. A memorial rally across France drew together more than three-and-a-half million people, about one-third of them in Paris, where nearly 50 world leaders joined them with linked arms in a show of international solidarity. Only later did some people begin to ask publicly about whether freedom of expression has limits when it is deeply offensive to others.

The *Charlie Hebdo* murders are a world away from the consulting room and potentially healing aspects of humour which are this book's main concern. But they remain a starkly exaggerated reminder that humour, like any other natural force, has its shadows and potential dangers as well as blessings. Trying to write at all about something so multi-faceted and subjective of definition is quite a task. Philosophers have been trying to pin it down for 2,000 years; ethnologists have explored it, historians have recorded it and sociologists observed it in action. If I had set out to read everything about humour and its manifestations in laughter that has been published in even the last decade, I would have had no time to write this book at all. And I might not have been very much the wiser, for anything as intensively subjective as humour will probably always evade categorical capture.

In trying to seek out a contemporary psychological story about humour, and relate it to some of the things that may go on in psychotherapists' consulting rooms, I have found myself paradoxically drawn along two paths that might seem to lead in the opposite direction: back into the historical past and back again into mythology. The first has helped me anchor the multiple, fleeting faces of humour for long enough to explore some of its different actions and find analogies and contrasts with what people find humorous now. As I've gone along, I've sometimes smiled in recognition, sometimes been shocked, and also become very aware of humour's shadow. I hope that readers too may find that the historical stories lead them to muse on their own senses of humour and how these may be expressed.

This historical slant has also touched on enduring psychological, even theological questions about human 'perfectibility' – about the mutability of psyche and the venerable and pervasive assumption that 'progress' is not just cultural but psychological. In her splendid study of laughter in ancient Rome, the classicist Mary Beard found this assumption already well in place; and she had not, she says, been able to discover a single culture which claimed to laugh more coarsely or crudely than those that went before.[5] So we may think, for instance, that we have culturally 'grown out of' the 'puerile' scatological humour of the Trickster, or of the Rabelaisian world of carnival, just as we assume that contemporary children will 'grow out of' their giggling fascination with bodies and their functions. But, as we'll see, both Jung and Bakhtin, in their very different ways, found such back-to-basics humour not only a constant layer in the individual and even cultural human unconscious, but a source of life-renewing energy as well. And don't we know it too? How many of us, if we're really honest, can resist the delightful incongruity of an 'inappropriate' fart?

As to the mythological path, I wasn't long into my explorations before I sensed some humorous spirit smirking at my efforts to pin things down, hiding my notes just as something seemed clear and blowing a raspberry at my pretensions. I suspect that even thinking about humour evokes Hermes, archetypal trickster, messenger to the gods, who travels effortlessly in his winged sandals and invisible cloak between upper and lower worlds and the hurly burly of life's marketplaces. Hermes was the god of boundaries: his phallic stone herms marked the borders between outside and inside, my place and yours. But he also was the very opposite: a shameless, inveterate thief, no respecter of boundaries at all. His very first act, not yet out of his cradle, was to steal his Brother Apollo's cattle. He nearly got away with it, snuggled back under his blanket, all wide-eyed innocence. Apollo reasoned it out of course, image as he is of the bright clarity of logical thought. Hermes cut him a deal: my tortoiseshell lyre for your cattle. Apollo grumpily accepted when Zeus, father of gods and men, intervened. But it was Hermes who got the better of it: he was the favourite, the one who made Zeus laugh.

That was far from the end of Hermes' story. In later times, the Romans called him Mercury, and he is as hard to grasp as quicksilver itself. The old alchemists saw him as the animating spirit Mercurius, both poison and panacea as he runs around the Earth enjoying equally the company of the good and the bad. For Jung, he was metaphor for the whole process of psychological work. Now you see him, now you don't. But he can also be a first class therapeutic guide, linking as he does the upper world of consciousness and the unconscious below as he moves through life's realities. So named or not, he will assuredly be in and out of these pages as we go along, as one personification of 'humour' itself.

Such mythic references are not just decorative. Through the years, I've had the good fortune to explore these old tales with very many groups of people, in Britain and well beyond. Each time is different from the last and the next. But each time, it seems to work. Something seems to animate us, the energy flows, we laugh and we enjoy ourselves. We also learn something more about human psychology and our own unique expression of it. Each person reacts differently to the tales, for in their sometimes seemingly wilful obscurity there is something for everyone, and nothing is either right or wrong. Participants may be true Jungian believers, curious sceptics or even sulky students under a three-line educational whip. The stories seem to cross national boundaries with as little effort as Hermes himself. I've enjoyed them with citizens of Belgrade and Bristol, Birmingham and Bangalore, Cambridge and Cape Town; they have animated groups in Russia, Bulgaria and international gatherings too.

Each time, one myth evokes another and we're enriched by the discovery of cross-cultural correspondences between them. Beneath and beyond all our individual and cultural differences, we seem to touch on something else: a humorous, even joyful, recognition of the infinite variety of common human experience. And, *pace* Apollo, we've got there not through analysis and rational deconstruction of the stories, for that would lead only to frustration. Their twists and turns, impossibly dream-like images and even flat self-contradictions, defy logic. We've been drawn instead from the realm of *logos* to that of *mythos*, from reading the stories in search of causal connections to letting them play with our imagination, from the ostensible, known world of consciousness to symbolic intimations of an unconscious that is individual and perhaps universal as well. So I hope that readers may find something of the same energy here, and that it draws them from my take on humour to discovering more about their own.

This evocation of myth has also given me a frame within which to work with humour's mercurial nature, its multiplicity of manifestations and its mockery of the fixed. The episodes of one particular myth and its afterlife run right through the book and help give it shape. The myth is both ancient and recognisably contemporary. It is the story about Demeter and Persephone, found in the *Homeric Hymns*; I hope my retelling retains its expression of enduring truths about human nature. This tale brings the airy, imaginative spirit of humour right back down to earth and into the body by balancing the evanescent Mercurius with the earthy Iambe/Baubo. As we go along, 'Iambe' will also emerge as a personification of humour; together, she and Hermes are a reminder of the relationship between mind, body and soul, in humour as in so many other aspects of being human. The story of Demeter and Persephone might seem far from humorous, beginning as it does in the devastation of loss. But it is also a story of the transformation of a grief that each of us may fearfully imagine into a hope for continuing life, creativity and fruitfulness. And it seems beautifully fit for this book's purpose, for the trigger for that seemingly impossible transformation was a joke.

The book has three main parts. The first is called Humour and the healers (Chapters 3–5). This begins with an exploration of how humour and psychotherapy have sat together among psychological theorists, from the founding parents onwards. From here, it gives something of the professional and public contexts in which therapists practise and, lastly, some speculations about what sort of people, humorous or not, they may tend to be. The second part is called What's so funny? (Chapters 6–8). This is what people often say when they just don't get the joke, and these three chapters are an invitation to readers to compare their own sense of humour with what has been thought humorous by philosophical theorists and plain people too, at different times and in different places. This particularly includes humour's darker aspects, and finally brings the whole subject back into the place where humour starts and is often manifest – the body and brain. Throughout, there's attention to where humour might help to develop psychological understanding. The final part is called In the consulting room (Chapters 9–12). Its concern is especially with long-running questions of just what the 'therapeutic relationship' might mean, and how humour might be a part of it; it includes at least something of what people on the receiving end have thought about this. It also explores more specifically whether humour has something to say about professionally familiar themes of therapeutic thresholds, power in the therapeutic relationship and boundaries. This part ends with a look at what's known about the place of laughter in communication and its possible implications for therapy.

Apart from this introductory chapter and a concluding coda, this book both starts and ends with an evocation of how humour can help humans to survive even the deepest sufferings and tragedies. As Chapter 13 shows, in the worst of contemporary imprisonments, when psychological energy is thrall to the dark underworld, when all hope seems dead, it may be humour that brings not just endurance but the renewal of life itself. Thousands of years ago, the story of Demeter, Persephone and Iambe was bringing that message too. And it's to that story we now turn.

Notes

1 Lindner vii.
2 Taylor.
3 Panksepp and Biven 154.
4 Midgeley 107–108.
5 Beard 68.

Chapter 2

A goddess laughs

It was beginning to get late. The girl had only gone across to the flower-meadow to picnic with her friends, she should have been home by now. The mother smiled: she must learn to stop this fussing. Only this morning she'd watched her girl run down the path, her easy young body already turning more awkward. It wouldn't be long before she was a woman, and out of the house for ever, leaving her mother's heart both rejoicing in her happiness and wrenched at the loss.

But not yet, surely: that was for the future. The mother turned up the lamps against the darkness of the night and her own imaginings. Then suddenly she heard her daughter scream out for her, a single cry stifled as if a great hand had clamped over her beautiful young mouth. A pain like no other pierced the mother's heart. She threw on her blue-black cloak and tore out of the house, grabbed a couple of torches from a startled road-side vendor and flew like a great bird across the land, darting and swooping as she looked and looked again for any trace of her girl. For nine days and nine nights she flew, asking and asking, never stopping to eat or drink, or even to wash her face. People crossed the road to avoid this filthy madwoman with her ceaseless questions. How could they have known that this was the Goddess Demeter herself, beloved for her gifts of golden corn and the bounty of harvests? They had enough to worry about: the unseasonal storms and deluges of the past nine days were already threatening their crops.

Even those who knew Demeter well didn't dare tell her about the rumours, until Hecate, guardian of the ways, at home in the dark, met her and confirmed that she too had heard the cry. Together, as the tenth day dawned, they flew to Helios the sun god, begging him to tell if his rays could illuminate the truth.

And so the dreadful story came out. Lord Zeus, the girl's own father, and his brother Hades, lord of the underworld, had together plotted to snatch her for Hades' bride. And Grandmother Gaia, Mother Earth herself, had connived with them, planting a beautiful glowing narcissus just where her own body opened to the underworld, knowing that the girl wouldn't be able to resist picking it. There was really nothing simpler: at that moment of delighted cupidity, the girl was snatched down into the great golden chariot of Hades with its four black horses, leaving only her anguished cry behind as the knowing earth closed once more.

So much betrayal! Not just by the brothers with whom Demeter had played and squabbled and laughed since they all had escaped their father Kronos, not just by her brother-husband Zeus, but by Grandmother Gaia herself, the very earth on which Demeter's own glorious harvests had so safely and unquestioningly relied. Now there was no refuge on earth or under the heavens. In a storm of rage and grief the goddess roamed the cities and the plains, one more old madwoman moaning and weeping and clenching her fist as she shouted curses to the sky.

And then the madness left her and only the exhausted weight of sorrow dragged her on. She found herself at the well at Eleusis where the city's young girls gathered and giggled as they drew their water. This was what her own Persephone should have been doing, joshing about the beautiful boy who'd just arrived in the neighbourhood, rolling her eyes at parental stupidities. Her sorrow sounded a sob so deep that it seemed the earth itself was shaken. The four lovely daughters of King Keleos dropped their bronze pitchers, frightened by this glimpse into an adult world they didn't want to enter. But, kindly girls, they couldn't just leave her there: they gingerly approached, asked where she came from, why she didn't seek lodgings with others of her age, gave her a run-down on the town. Demeter wasn't ready to reveal herself; she had never felt less of a goddess's power. So she told them an adventure-story, the sort that had widened Persephone's eyes with glee when she was safely tucked up in bed. She told them how she'd been forcibly and violently snatched by Cretan pirates, but managed to escape before they could sell her, and wandered until she'd ended up here. Rubbish really, but how she wished that it was her daughter's story too, that Persephone had escaped her bondage and wandered to the well and into her mother's arms. She had a sudden memory of her daughter's baby body, her sunny smell. And she heard herself asking the girls if they knew of anyone who needed a nanny for a new-born.

The daughters of Keleos brightened. Truth to tell, they were feeling a bit out of their depth here; there was something quite awesome in this old woman. As it happened, they said, their own mother, Queen Metaneira, had just had a baby boy and needed a nanny right now. They raced home to tell the story, speeding to pass responsibility back to the adult world. And before long they returned to bring the strange old woman to the palace.

As the goddess crossed the threshold, the queen was awestruck, drawn into a radiance that filled the doorway with its energy. Hastily she offered the old woman her own regal couch. But Demeter just stood silent, her eyes cast down, until the servant Iambe, who seemed instantly to know what she needed, offered her a stool. And there the old woman sat, silent still, her face veiled, her sorrow casting a blue-black shadow over this cheerful household. They tried to engage her in conversation, tempt her with different foods and drinks. But nothing moved her; it seemed she could sit there until she died of grief.

Then everything changed. Iambe limped up to her, looked her right in the eye and told her a joke. The queen and her daughters froze. But Demeter smiled, and then she laughed and then everyone laughed for sheer relief. The queen poured a celebratory glass of the best red wine. But the goddess at last ended her silence to ask instead for water mixed with barley meal and mint. And so she broke her fast.

The old woman's laugh, and the breaking of her fast, lifted the atmosphere. Queen Metaneira felt herself again, accustomed to command. She was more than ever convinced that this mysterious visitor was someone who impelled respect. How else could she have proposed to entrust the stranger with her son, born when all hope of another child had past? The old woman was glad, she said, to take on this precious task. When she added that she would protect the boy from witchcraft with strong safeguards of her own, somehow it didn't sound like an exaggeration. So it was settled, and Iambe led the old nurse to her quarters. Already there was an ease between them, a mutual memory of that joke. As time went on, the other servants got used to the way these two went about together; sometimes the sound of their laughter arrived before them.

The boy grew in the goddess's care, straight and tall beyond his years, so beautiful that people were only half joking when they said he could be divine. And no wonder, for every time Demeter looked at him and touched him, she remembered the babyhood of her own lost girl. And she determined that this child she would never lose, that she would make him as ageless and deathless as a god. So she breathed sweetness into his lovely body and anointed him with ambrosia, and every night, when everyone else had gone to bed, she buried him in the heart of the fire. Who knows what would have become of him if one night the queen hadn't happened to leave her bed and seen him burning there, just as if he'd been a torch? She screamed. Demeter looked up. She snatched the child from the fire and threw him to the ground. She raged at the terrified mother, told her she was a fool and had ruined everything. Now her beautiful son would die like any mortal, caught up in a civil war that would ravage this beautiful country. This was no old nurse speaking. Now at last she revealed herself. This, she declared, was the word of Demeter, the immortal goddess, who had been the greatest blessing and source of joy for mortals and immortals alike.

The household, alerted by the din to cluster in the hall, froze in awestruck terror. The moment seemed interminable. And then, something changed. Did Iambe come to the goddess's side to calm her fury? Demeter seemed to recollect herself. 'Come now', she said. 'Come now' – as much to herself perhaps as to the queen, who still cowered so fearfully that she hadn't even picked up her screaming boy. Summon the people, Demeter commanded, and build a great temple. She herself, she promised, would inaugurate her Mysteries there. And as these were performed in all purity, she would reconcile the people to her heart. With that command and that promise, the goddess revealed herself in all her shining beauty, so glorious that even after she had left the house its darkest corners shimmered with light.

But then all became dark again. Once parted from her lovely boy, the goddess was once more consumed by grief for her lost daughter. She sat immobile in the great temple that the people of Eleusis had so hastily built her, wrapped again in her blue-black cloak. Her grief created a most cruel year. The farmers were helpless. They wearily yoked their oxen yet once more, and ploughed again and again. They scattered and rescattered their barley and seed, but whatever they did, nothing grew. Even the gods became anxious. If this went on, the whole race of human beings would surely perish. And then who would honour them with gifts and sacrifices? Zeus tried to call Demeter back home to Olympus. But she was adamant. Not one foot would she set on the sacred mountain, not one blade of grass would she allow to grow on earth until she was reunited with her girl. Zeus knew this mood; she'd been obdurate even as a child. There was nothing else for it. He sent Hermes down to Hades, right into the underworld, with a message that he must send his bride up to her mother. So the great golden chariot with its four black horses was made ready, and Hermes drove Persephone up and on through the vast distances, until he drew up with a flourish in front of Demeter's temple at Eleusis. When she saw her girl, the goddess leapt for joy. The two of them embraced and laughed and cried and hugged again as if they could never be parted. But they could be and they were.

For all the time she had been in Hades' kingdom, Persephone had never eaten a morsel of food; she had never so bound herself to her husband and his realm. But Hades was stealthy. When she was preparing for her return to earth, distracted by joy and excitement, he had slipped just one pomegranate seed into her mouth and caught her off guard. Just one seed – but it was enough to seal the marriage. So Demeter knew that a deal had to be struck with the gods. This is what she proposed: for a third of the year, Persephone would live with her underworld lord, and whenever the spring flowers started to appear, she would return to her mother until the earth became dormant again. Zeus gave the plan his nod and straightway Demeter made the earth burst into leaves and flowers to seal the bargain. The arrangement endured and is encoded even now in the seasons of the year.

Now, finally, the goddess could keep her promise. She inaugurated her Mysteries in her temple at Eleusis and so powerful were they that pilgrims came to them from all over the known world. Participants were enjoined never to profane the rite by speaking of it, and though they lasted for 2,000 years, to this day nobody knows exactly what the Mysteries entailed. But what we do know is that they evoked the story of Demeter and Persephone and the great cycle of life, death and rebirth which is still both the rhythm of the earth and the hope of countless human hearts. Some say that at the holiest moment, Iambe was right there.

The story of Demeter and Persephone has been mined for a multiplicity of meanings and insights into psychological life. But one thing seems certain: without Iambe's initial joke and the goddess's answering laugh, the story could not have unfolded at all. At that moment, the world was saved from the consequences of Demeter's anguish, from empty fields and dying animals, and famine among humankind. The goddess was brought back to herself as nurturer of life, even as the drink of barley meal and mint she commanded already hinted at the rituals of the Mysteries which also encompass death and regeneration. Humans in the depths of grief and depression may have no faith in that continuing natural cycle. For them, there may only be the endurance of empty barrenness, and a belief that creative life is dead. But what the story tells is that once we can be touched by humour, even the most barren, deadly times can pass. At that moment, there is a coming together of body, mind and soul, and a reconnection with the natural, inbuilt capacity for psychological growth and fruitful creativity.

The flow of life may be fitful, as the story tells. Demeter's grief and anger was not easily assuaged. Yet at two key points – the surrendering of first the boy and then of her possessive longing for her daughter – she yielded. The goddess could surely have insisted on keeping the lovely boy in whom she had found so much consolation. The Olympians were not known for their sensitivity to human feeling. But instead there is that extraordinary pause, that moment of reflection. 'Come now', says the goddess, 'come now'. Then there could be a restoration of the necessary boundaries between the human and the divine, as the child was returned to his human fate. Then too Demeter could recall her essential nature as a source of greatest blessing and joy, and could move from fury at the insult to her dignity to the promise of reconciliation. Humans too can move from depression to a compensatory inflation, an identification with 'divine' or archetypal inner energies. Then humour can bring that moment of wry self-reflection, the step back from engulfing emotion that restores proportion. 'Come now', we can say to our inflation. When we stop taking ourselves quite so seriously, we can start to take ourselves seriously enough. And then perhaps we can begin to take others seriously enough as well. We can imagine a moment of empathy between goddess and queen, a communication between mothers' hearts, as Meteneira's fear and grief reminds Demeter of the sharpness of her own first anguish. In the depths of depression and grief, there is no room for the other. Humour can bring people together in a shared humanity.

The story tells too what that might come to mean. Even the goddess must learn that there are limits to her power. But it's from her negotiation with the rulers of heaven and the underworld that the great cycle of the seasons is born, and the central mystery of creation becomes accessible to human consciousness through the great Mysteries of Eleusis. Individual lives have their seasons too, encompassing not just the great beginnings and finalities, but also the everyday births and deaths of hope and disappointment, and renewals of aspiration and fulfilment. As Demeter's story unfolded, we're told, the goddess kept Iambe by her side. In the individual unfoldings of the universal human story too, humour can be life's good companion.

Humour and the healers

Chapter 3

In theory

The British psychoanalyst Peter Lomas thought that the persona of therapists bore traces of the restrictive and life-denying elements of organised religion; when they lectured, he caught an echo of the well-modulated cadences of the priest. Colleagues could feel the same about seminars: they wished, they told him, that they didn't feel they were in church. Nina Coltart, another of the most accessible British psychoanalysts of her time, made no bones about the 'turgid, pompously theatrical and quite boring' tone of much analytic writing. Her own was mercifully different: she wanted it to be not shallow but light-hearted – and she succeeded. Perhaps it's not surprising that both Lomas and Coltart left the British Psychoanalytical Society. But even she balked at writing a paper about humour in psychoanalysis. 'I suppose', she wrote,

> there is a fear that I may be deluding myself, or not noticing that what it really means is that my technique has got sloppy, or that I have developed a special sort of defence, or both, or many more horrendous things.[1]

A professional generation later, how much has changed? If most people would bless their sense of humour for enabling them to keep their grip on sanity, it can seem that psychotherapy doesn't share their view. At one end of the therapeutic spectrum, Adam Phillips, writer and psychoanalyst, examines with great cleverness the process of *Going Sane*, of reaching that elusive state defined almost entirely by its opposite. But the 'deep sanity' he's concerned with has nothing comedic in its appreciations of life's realities. Unlike the slightly comic 'superficially sane', his deeply sane are 'rather more like tragic heroes and heroines who have survived their ordeals', seeking even their pleasures, one suspects, with a sense of ironic detachment.[2] At the other end of the spectrum, in her School of Life handbook boldly titled *How to Stay Sane*, psychotherapist and writer Philippa Perry offers many useful self-help exercises for enhanced self-observation, better relating to others, dealing with stress and reassessing our fixed stories about ourselves. But there is nothing here either about how humour might oil the wheels of reflection and relationship.

Nor does this seem to be a uniquely British business. In his much re-printed primer *On Being a Therapist*, Jeffrey Kottler, professor in the department of counselling at California State University, lists the qualities of the ideal: quiet confidence, wise expertise, perception and sensitivity, stability and grounding, patience, self-discipline. To be sure, a contagious zest for life and spontaneity and playfulness also figure. But humour comes in among the 'alsos' at the end of the list, together with creativity, flexibility, honesty and sincerity.[3] The clinical writings of Irvin Yalom, the veteran American existential psychiatrist, seem to radiate these last qualities. (And his *Lying on the Couch* is surely the funniest and cleverest novel ever written about the nature and ethics of the therapeutic relationship.) In the stories he tells in *Love's Executioner*, Yalom shirks nothing of his patients' pain and distress, but there is nothing solemn either in his wryly humorous observation of them, himself and their interactions. Even he, however, in his more recent *The Gift of Therapy*, 'an open letter to a new generation of therapists and their patients', makes no mention of a sense of life's humour as something worth cultivating, for everyone concerned.

Yet humour has been encoded in us humans from the start. Some say that God laughed for six days as he created the world, and on the seventh he both laughed and cried and the soul came into it. In another beginning of things, Sarah and Abraham laughed when the Lord told them that they would have a child in their great old age. But so they did and they called him Isaac, which means 'he laughs'. So laughter came into the world. And, hard won, here it remained when God rewarded Abraham's faith by finally refusing the boy as sacrifice, so allowing laughter to pass into human DNA for ever. Depth psychology has its own mythic beginnings. Freud thought that our smile first comes into the world when we are satisfied and sated babies at our mother's breast, and the French psychoanalyst Janine Chasseguet-Smirgel proposed that it is through humour that the human being can banish the terror of the loss of love, by trying to be their own loving mother. On the other side of the channel, the psychoanalyst Christopher Bollas has wondered whether it isn't humour that precedes our very sense of self and the world. Perhaps the first other an infant sees, he suggests, is a clown: the eye-widening, exaggerating, smiling, grimacing mother who 'cracks up' with her baby's fragmentary experience, and so transforms potential trauma by turning it into pleasure, equipping the child to deal with the heedless, uncontrollable real world in which they will one day have to live. 'Perhaps a sense of humour is essential to human survival', muses Bollas.

> Amusement in oneself and in the other may be a vital constituent part of a comprehensive perspective on life. The mother who develops her baby's sense of humour is assisting him to detach from dire mere existence, from simply being in the rather shitty world of infancy, for example. Such a child can, as an adult, ultimately find humour in the most awful circumstances, benefiting from the origins of the comic sense.[4]

If humour is a gift so intrinsic to human wellbeing and survival, it does seem rather odd that more of us aren't writing about it, rejoicing in it in our professional meetings and relationships and learning more about it. There is nothing in our ancestry that forbids its welcome. There is plenty of humour in the writings of Freud and Jung, radically different though these are. Freud was famously fond of a joke, especially a Jewish one. *The Interpretation of Dreams* is full of jokes too many altogether, fretted his friend Wilhelm Fleiss. Five years later, Freud devoted a whole volume to them, and he was not averse to a joke in the consulting room either. He once told his young patient Dora of a 'very entertaining moment' when another female patient had asked him to open a little ivory box that she always carried with her and take out a sweet. 'She did not calm down until I had pointed out to her with a laugh how well her words were adapted to quite another meaning.' Young Dora was already battling with Freud's insistence on finding sexual meaning and motivation pretty well everywhere in her life. (Indeed, many of her exchanges with him could be re-cast as pantomimic parody: 'Oh no I didn't' – 'Oh yes you did'.) Just what she made of this 'very entertaining moment' we're not told. But many years later, his loving patient HD, the American poet Hilda Doolittle, recalled fondly his ironical manner, his mouth that always seemed slightly to smile.[5]

Outside the consulting room too, Freud's witty, barbed humour is often remembered. His grandson Clement had a nice story of walking hand in hand with this benign, cigar-scented companion in Vienna and coming across a crowd gathered around a man who had fallen in a dramatic epileptic fit. His hat had fallen off, and some passers-by were throwing in sympathetic coins. When the little boy asked his grandfather why he too didn't give the poor man some money, Freud answered dryly 'He did not do it well enough.' Even through the sufferings and tragedies of his last years, his humour didn't leave him; it's tempting to think that it was this that gave him the capacity to endure the pain of illness and exile. As a condition for an exit visa from Nazi Vienna he had to sign a declaration that he had been treated with the utmost respect by the authorities, that he had no grounds at all for any complaint. Of course he had to sign, even though his home had been invaded, his possessions duffed over and his daughter Anna hauled into custody for questioning. But he added his own postscript to the document: 'I can heartily recommend the Gestapo to anyone.' And when it was discovered that the invaders had raided the safe for the family's passports and quite an amount of money, 'Dear me', he remarked, 'I have never taken so much for a single session.'[6]

Jung's sense of humour could hardly have been more different, not so much an ironic smile as a great guffaw. (One of history's unanswered questions: would their inevitable parting have been as bitter and personally wounding if they had had a shared SOH?) Jung didn't write about humour directly, apart perhaps from in his essay on the trickster archetype. But he was fond of quoting Schopenhauer's dictum that it was the one human attribute that allows us to possess our soul in freedom. He once told Marie Louise von Franz, his devoted disciple, that he made a great point of seeing whether potential patients had a sense of humour; without it, he thought, they would be very difficult to work with. And when people remember Jung, it's rarely without the accompaniment of his uproarious and infectious laugh, his sheer *joie de vivre* and enjoyment of jokes of all kinds, the earthier the better. His admirer Laurens van der Post describes Jung's laugh as a sound so uninhibited and total that it stopped strangers in their tracks.

> Both Olympian and intensely human, it was a laughter possible only to those blessed with some of the insights of the gods themselves ... an expression of sheer joy at the restoration of proportion, of the triumph in the significance of the small over the unreality of excess and disproportion in the established and great.[7]

This puncturing of pomposity and persona went far, and was sometimes far from comfortable for those on the receiving end. Jung's biographer Deirdre Bair tells of a toe-curling game called Alleluiah, in which he made the participants throw between them a large handkerchief, all the while shouting personal confessions or something embarrassing or accusatory about the person at whom the handkerchief was aimed. The largely introverted participants hated it and it did nothing at all to foster good humour among them. But Jung enjoyed it, so they couldn't sit it out. At the end of his life, in an unpublished draft of the memoir that was to be bowdlerised into *Memories, Dreams, Reflections*, Jung called this sort of thing *Shadenfroh*, enjoyment of the troubles of others. He loved pulling people's legs and found it boring when others didn't share his fun. He wasn't above playing tricks on his children either, or encouraging them to laugh at his mistress Toni Wolff's ineptitude in the kitchen. Behind the humorous and kindly old man of John Freeman's famous *Face to Face* television interview, Jung's humour has another aspect – a reminder that this, like any psychological energy, has a dark side too, from which he didn't shirk.[8]

So humour was far from taboo at depth psychology's beginnings. But if its first inspirations were to survive as any more than the insights of two great minds and their immediate followers, the teachings had to be codified into a coherent body of understanding and a standard enough way of applying it. The search was on for alchemical *coagulatio*, for the fixities of reliable theory and technique. Humour is no obvious help at all here: it works for the very antithesis. Its delight in turning the known world on its head, blowing raspberries at authority, alerting us to over-rigid perspectives, is all about *dissolutio*, dissolving certainties so they can be thought anew. And when the aspiration is to create a standardisation of 'technique', a predictably effective way for psychotherapists to relate to their patients, then humour's ambiguities may seem positively dangerous. When emotional suffering and distress stifles the patient's capacity for humour, then therapists may well tread softly indeed, for fear of being misperceived as mocking and cruel.

Not hard, then, to see how in the development of depth psychology and its derivatives, humour might well get left behind. Freud was famously unamused by any deviation from his creed; followers who played with his tenets were banished and disowned. His own changing ambitions for psychoanalysis can offer a snapshot of what this would lead to. Back at its first stirrings, he was often asked by his intelligent young woman patients how he proposed to help them, given that he could do nothing about the intellectual and social restrictions of their lives to which he related their hysterical illnesses. No doubt, he said, fate would be better able than he to relieve them.

> But you will be able to convince yourself that much will be gained if we succeed in transforming your hysterical misery into common unhappiness. With a mental life that has been restored to health, you will be better armed against that unhappiness.

As time went on Freud modified this stoic creed. In 1904, he was able to say that the aim of his therapy was 'the practical recovery of the patient, the restoration of his ability to lead an active life and his *capacity for enjoyment*' (my italics). But by the end of his life, such lively possibility had contracted into the dryness of theory: 'the business of the analysis is to secure the best possible psychological conditions for the function of the ego; with that it has discharged its task'.[9]

Freud's theory was precious to its adherents. The Controversial Discussions that racked the British psychoanalytical community after his death must seem frankly incomprehensible, even risible, to anyone outside the fold. But for the followers of Anna Freud's implacable defence of her father and the adherents of the apostate Melanie Klein as they battled it out, there was nothing at all to laugh about. Both principals inevitably brought their own baggage to the fray. The roots of Melanie Klein's tumultuous personal life could perhaps, thought her biographer, be traced to childhood in a family 'riddled with guilt, envy, and occasionally explosive rages, and infused with strong incestuous overtones'. Freud loved his last-born Annerl's childhood naughtiness, but she was destined to carry the weight of his mantle until the end of her days, when her tiny figure was pushed on wheelchair outings wrapped in his woollen great-coat. Clement Freud's awe-tinged childhood liking for his Aunt Anna cooled as he grew up. Once, thinking it might entertain her, he showed her the results of a competition in the *New Statesman* magazine, which invited readers to summarise the last conversation between an analyst and their patient after three years of meetings. One of the winners was brief: 'Goodbye. I made it all up.' Anna was not amused. As she read it, the lines on her forehead deepened. 'The patient', she said, 'was not cured.'[10]

John Bowlby, who was there, thought the main protagonists in the Controversial Discussions were mirror images of each other, stubborn women who refused to open their minds to the ideas of others. Their followers, he said, were presented with a single choice: to worship at the shrine of either St Sigmund or St Melanie. It was only in old age that either woman could find a humour that might – who knows? – have made their struggles less closed-minded and intense.

Anna Freud's biographer saw her as forever torn between caution and adventure, a super-conscientious dedication and 'islands of fantasy and handicrafts', never able in her youth to find a way by humour through the tension; it was only in old age that she could joke about how to find inner reconciliation. People who knew Melanie Klein late in her life remembered her ringing laugh, but earlier it was the strength of her ambition and her hugely controlling nature that were most often remarked. A.S. Neil, the radical educationalist, remembered a wedding at which many of Klein's followers were also guests. 'They can't laugh. Melanie has evidently shown them humour is a complex which no normal man should have.' Decades later, a dedicated defence of the purity of Freudian doctrine could still be as taxing, as Janet Malcolm showed for all time in her brilliant analysis of *The Impossible Profession*, seen through the anguished eyes of the New York psychoanalyst she called 'Aaron Green'. For him, it appears, every professional interaction, almost every session and perhaps even every interpretation seemed like walking on eggshells lest he deviate from the truth of his calling.[11]

Jung's approach to psychology reads very differently from Freud's. His writings are peppered with warnings against taking his ideas too seriously, at the expense of the truth of individual experience.

> If you begin the analysis with a fixed belief in some theory which purports to know all about the nature of neurosis, you apparently make your task very much easier; but you are nevertheless in danger of riding roughshod over the real psychology of your patient and of disregarding his individuality.

Theories could never be more than a helpful backup to the work. 'As soon as a dogma is made of them, it is evident that an inner doubt is being stifled. One could as little catch the psyche in a theory as one could catch the world.' And as he said time and again, no theory could be definitive, for each was bound to reflect the psychological makeup of its holder. He went further: we can never say anything *about* psyche, for psyche is always speaking about itself. 'Thank God I am not a Jungian!' he reportedly exclaimed. He attracted passionate acolytes, yet he was not always kind about the 'eleven thousand virgins' who clustered so adoringly around him. For him, what seemed to matter most was not that people followed some theory, but that each one sought their own path of 'individuation', becoming more fully their unique self.[12]

That said, of course Jung had overall 'theories' about the workings of psyche, and towards the end of his life he could sound bitter that they had not been more widely taken up. The stories about his dominance of the Zurich Analytical Club on which he so often tried out his ideas suggest that the rhetoric may perhaps be best taken with a pinch of salt. When the C.G. Jung Institute was finally established in Zurich to further his teaching, he made very sure of the composition of its board – and to make assurance doubly sure, proposed that its members should be 'elected' for life. ('Like Stalin, omnipotent! Selected for a lifetime! It is impossible to do anything against them', fulminated his redoubtable junior colleague Jolande Jacobi.) But all the same, the logic of Jung's central tenet, that all human experience is based on the finally unknowable archetypes of the deep collective unconscious, had to preclude any attempt at fixity of theory or practice. And even when he was tetchily defending his ideas, his humour could save him. One visitor to the Zurich Analytical Club remembers his eruption after a lecture: 'How can you offer these things as new findings? That's something I have already said a hundred years ago!' But then he was the first to burst out laughing. While Freudians suffered their Controversial Discussions, Jungians could enjoy the Eranos conferences, in which thinkers from many disciplines together explored the human psyche's infinite expressions.[13]

From the very differing accounts of those who worked with him, Jung was true to his own dictum that each patient needed a 'theory' of their own. One recalls a session almost entirely taken up by his expounding of his ideas; another, deeply depressed, remembers that she sat with him in silence for the hour, during which he did no more than occasionally reach out to stroke her arm or pat her hand until she finally found peace. Joe Henderson, who became the grand old man of Jungian psychology in San Francisco until his death at the age of 104, recalled that Jung would pace about and talk of everything that came into his ever-fertile mind – a personal memory, a dream, an allegorical story or a joke; yet he could also be quiet, serious, extremely personal, making life-changing observations indirectly 'as if they were to be accepted lightly – even joyously'. Mary Briner, another of his analysands, wrote to him, by now in his 80s, proposing that she publish her diary of their work so many years before, as an account of his 'method'. He was outraged: 'I have no method at all, when it comes to the individual case.' For him, each analysis was a meeting of two individuals in their conscious and unconscious totalities. 'So you're in the soup too!' was his opening remark to Jane Wheelwright. She, Henderson and Briner inevitably carried their experience of analysis into their own therapeutic practices; in their filmed reminiscences a very long time later, they positively crackled with humour and enjoyment of both the life-changing importance and manifold absurdities of life in the Zurich soup.[14]

Whether Freudian or Jungian, both or neither, the soup is what depth psychotherapists are bound to be in. Each of us starts from a belief in the existence of something called 'the unconscious'; however we define it, we work hard to help people explore its ways and so lessen the painful mismatches between who they consciously think they are and what else may be going on. But here's the joke: *we don't really know what we're talking about.* 'The unconscious' has to be just that – finally unknowable, inaccessible to the conscious mind. The whole edifice of competing theories and techniques is built on differing myths, woven to find meaning in the human condition according to the psychological makeup of their weavers.

This doesn't make them any the less true. Myths, thought Jung, were 'original revelations of the preconscious psyche, involuntary statements about unconscious psychic happenings', 'first and foremost psychic phenomena that reveal the nature of the soul'. The very etymology of the word gives a clue about the necessarily mythic nature of depth psychology, striving as it impossibly does to understand the finally incomprehensible. *Mythos* is 'the true speech – speech about that which is'. This spoken truth is the opposite of *logos*, which came to be associated with writing, and all the causal and sequential ordering that came with it. (Think, perhaps, of the difference between a dream first sleepily remembered, with all its jostling simultaneity of imagery and event, and a dream written down, the jostle now ordered by the conscious mind into a linear narrative that 'makes sense'.) A second etymology associates 'myth' with '*musteion*', which is associated with 'mystery' and means 'to close the eyes or mouth'. So myth is to do with 'that which cannot be seen or spoken'. If we play with these two meanings, we can arrive at *an utterance about that which cannot be spoken*, and *a true speech about that which cannot be seen or understood*. I can't think of a better description of the conscious ego's attempts to articulate the unconscious, or indeed of the work of psychotherapy itself.[15]

The joke's on us and either we get it, or we don't. We can try to embrace the radical uncertainty of our endeavours, compelled by our nature to try to understand what it means to be human even as we smile wryly, even laugh, at the impossibility of the task. Or we can redouble our efforts to resolve the intolerable paradox by clinging to our preferred theory, forever stretching the *logos* of our conscious understandings in pursuit of a final 'truth'. Neither approach is either right or wrong, except perhaps in our own minds. In the end, the choice is simply an expression of who we are. For me, a capacity to accept, even embrace, paradox as the very structure of our own multiple and often contradictory selves, does seem one of the most important tools for living a humorous life. For you, the pursuit of greater certainties may offer a far sturdier toolkit than that.

Some people live more comfortably with uncertainty; others seek a firmer structure to their lives. The first sort might be expected to be drawn to Jung's ideas, inspired by his own scepticism about fixed theories, his radical willingness to expose himself to the unknown, his delving into ever-wider metaphorical correspondences for hints about the archetypal essentials of human nature. For him, there could be no certainties: everything was 'both–and' rather than 'either–or', a continual dance of psychic opposites. No good looking here then for a guardian of certainty. Yet there are Jungian zealots too, defending their true faith against the influential 'post-Jungians' who seek their own certainties by embracing the more certain theories and techniques of psychoanalysis. And yet again, it is a psychoanalyst who has pinpointed a joke that runs alongside the seriousness of our endeavours. Too much is made, thinks Christopher Bollas, certainly in Protestant England, of the essential sufferings of a psychoanalysis. But this is not the only way to characterise its structure.

> Throughout, the analysand's speech undermines his authority: the mere fact of free association deconstructs any tragic hero's destiny.... [E]ach session has an ironic fate: one begins with a notion of what one is going to talk

about, only to discover that speaking dismantles intention and brings up unexpected material.... [T]he parapraxal self speaks in an absurd space, and psychoanalysis is a comic structure: the analysand is turned upside down by the intrinsic subversions of unconsciously driven speech. A patient in analysis is straight man to his unconscious and it is a long time, if ever, before he comes to enjoy the comedy. This is true of life in general. Fortunately, psychoanalysis knows this and gives the patient a couch, no doubt so that he can lie down before he slips and falls.[16]

Ouch?

Notes

References to Jung's *Collected Works* are by volume number and paragraph; those to Freud's *Standard Edition* by volume and page.

1 Lomas 34; Coltart, *Freely Associated* 165; Coltart, *Slouching* 11–12.
2 Phillips, *Going Sane* 224.
3 Kottler 36–37.
4 Freud, 'Jokes' VIII:146; Bollas, *Cracking Up* 244.
5 Freud, 'Fragment' VII:77; H.D. 92, 78.
6 Clement Freud 26; Ernest Jones 3, 241; Martin Freud 211.
7 Von Franz 183; van der Post 48–49.
8 Bair 312, 753, 317, 319.
9 Freud and Breuer, *Hysteria*, 323; Freud 'Psychoanalytic Procedure' VII:253; Freud 'Analysis Terminable' XXIII:250.
10 Grosskurth 20; Clement Freud 27.
11 Bowlby in Grosskurth 325; Young-Bruehl 419; Neil in Grosskurth 448.
12 Jung, 'Analytical Psychology and Education' 17:181; 'Medicine and Psychotherapy' 16:198; 'Trickster Figure' 9i:483.
13 Jacobi in Bair 532; Fierz 20.
14 Henderson in Bair 379; Briner in Bair 382; Wheelwright 103; 'Filmed reminiscences' in *Matter of Heart*.
15 Jung, 'Child Archetype' 9i:261; 'Archetypes' 9i: 7; Otto 29; Armstrong 6.
16 Bollas, *Cracking Up* 224.

Chapter 4
Looking outwards

In 1971, the American psychiatrist and psychoanalyst Lawrence S. Kubie issued a warning to any colleague who was even thinking of raising a smile.

> Humor blunts the vigilance of our self-observing mechanisms and our self-correction efforts.... Over the patient's desperation, the therapist's humor runs a steam-roller. I have picked up traces of a patient's delayed, bitter responses to the light-hearted or bantering approach of the therapist more often than I care to contemplate.... I cannot point to a single patient in whose treatment humor proved to be a safe, valuable and necessary aid.[1]

Kubie's influential article was reprinted in 1994 in an American collection called *The Use of Humor in Psychotherapy*. The editor, Herbert S. Strean, believed this to be the very first book to address the subject, and proudly hailed his contributors as 'unique individuals': 'they have had the courage to investigate a most contentious issue that has been shrouded in secrecy'.[2] When you consider that investigating the secret-shrouded is the very stuff of psychoanalytic practice, this gives humour (and humor) power indeed.

Strean's own starting point was clear. 'It is a virtual truism [*sic*] that it is the relatively mature and emotionally healthy individual who laughs frequently and enjoys it.' Mental health professionals, he said, tended to agree that the absence of a sense of humour, like an inability to cry, indicated that someone was suffering from emotional conflicts and was probably depressed. But as he pointed out, psychoanalysts had been far more interested in the inability to mourn than the inability to laugh. Indeed, their attitude to the very idea of potential therapeutic value in laughter could even be called phobic: laughter had been both decried and demeaned as 'acting out, resisting, regressive transference, maladaptive response and frequently a disguised way of expressing hostility'.[3]

Strean's contributors were certainly aware of the dangers. The therapist's laughter, they warned, could cloak an aggressive belittling of the patient; it could be both defensive and irrelevant, used merely for the therapist's own narcissistic gratification. Its premature use, thought one, was rather like premature ejaculation – only unilaterally and partially gratifying, and in the long run disastrous for the whole enterprise. But laughter could also, some thought, smuggle in uncomfortable truths and help people to express their feelings and mobilise a more robust attitude to their troubles. A shared laugh could also bring a profound moment of human connection to a patient caught in the isolation of suffering. 'There is a moment in laughter', said one contributor, 'when the laughers' eyes meet and for a moment, they are not alone. There is a shared, sometimes very intimate message: "I know exactly where you are. I've been there too".' And even if, as another thought, the only effective jokes in analysis were the ones which poked fun at the analyst, then they had value too, as they offered a clue to the patient's all-important attitude to parental figures.[4]

For the likes of 'Aaron Green' and his doctrinally pure colleagues at the New York Psychoanalytic Institute, this sort of thing would have been unlikely, I suspect, to go down well. For a start, several of the contributors to Strean's book were on the faculty of the New York Center for Psychoanalytic Training and Research at Columbia University, set up in 1945 after a savage schism with the Institute; indeed, Strean himself was its Director. Nearly 40 years later, as Janet Malcolm found, Green had nothing but bitterness and scorn for this apostate body. '"But the schism was years ago", I said. "What's the matter with them now?" Aaron frowned, and said in a dark, low voice, "They're sharp dressers." I laughed. "Is that all?" "Isn't that enough?" Aaron said.' He laughed too. But he went on to tell a story about how one day, shortly after he'd finished his training, he bought himself a herringbone tweed jacket. He really enjoyed that jacket, he felt great every time he wore it. Only two years later did he realise why: it was exactly the jacket most favoured by his colleagues at the Institute, in effect its uniform. No one had to teach them how analysts should dress. Consciously or unconsciously, they learned the lesson, just as they learned what psychoanalysis 'was' and the unalterable rules by which they must practice it.[5]

Thirty years on, who knows how much humour has managed to creep into consulting rooms, either at the New York Psychoanalytic Institute or elsewhere? The versions of what happens behind those doors that make their way into professional meetings and publications are so heavily disguised for anonymity, so selected to make a theoretical point, that the real flavour of any therapeutic moment can perhaps hardly be conveyed. To catch the feeling of a shared wry smile, a good joke, the pun of a moment's association or a liberating splutter may seem so difficult that it's simply left out. But another reason for omission might be that it's still not seen as a part of 'proper' practice, or that colleagues still, as Nina Coltart feared all those years ago, might frown.

Twenty years after its original publication, Strean's volume was being reprinted – which at least suggests that the debate about a place for humour in psychotherapy is not over yet. Some might feel that it has hardly yet begun. In 2013, Steven M. Sultanoff, psychologist and past president of the American Association for Applied and Therapeutic Humor, reported on how far his field had come. He found stories enough of humour in the consulting room, but most were simply anecdotal; there had been very little theoretical discussion or empirical evidence to support humour's more systematic use. Yet, as Sultanoff summarises, there's research already to indicate that humour can have a therapeutic effect on biochemistry, emotions, behaviours and cognitions. When people laugh, their levels of stress hormones go down and of antibodies go up; cardiovascular, muscular and skeletal body systems are all activated or exercised. Humour can relieve depression, reduce the impact of stressful events and anxiety, and help people to discharge pent-up feelings and become more creative problem-solvers. It can foster connection with others: those who experience their family doctors as humorous, for instance, are less likely to sue. This last may have important implications for psychotherapists, and not just for their pocketbooks: humour can strengthen the therapeutic alliance, which for over 50 years has been reckoned to have more effect on patient change than any other factor.

So what makes humour therapeutic and how do practitioners foster it? These rather key questions remain unanswered, but Sultanoff suggests a working frame. For him, humour is therapeutic if it is purposefully used for the client's benefit, and its outcome enhances the client's health or facilitates healing or coping, whether physical, emotional, social or cognitive. Therapists need to add 'humour skills' to their toolkit, expanding their vision of the comic and learning how to tickle their clients' funny bones. They need to embody three classic therapeutic virtues: empathy, genuineness and acceptance of their clients. If they can convey these, their clients will be more likely to experience their humour as caring and compassionate, a 'real' expression of who they are, and benign in its intent. For their part, those on the receiving end must be able to appreciate the incongruity, ludicrousness or ridiculousness that makes the intervention a humorous one. This is not likely if they are so steeped in their distress that they cannot even for this moment step outside it.

In short, though Sultanoff doesn't put it like this, be kindly, gauge your audience and watch your timing. The trouble with such sensible advice is that it might seem a bit too ordinary for many depth psychologists, a bit too like normal, decent behaviour towards people who feel very unhappy. Depth psychologists have learned to see psychological life and relationships – including those between their patients and themselves – as extraordinarily complicated processes which they can only begin to understand after years of self-examination and study. Even then, they can never be sure they've got it right. For people who see life like this, humour is unlikely to be more straightforward than any other communication, and its possible therapeutic use will have to be hedged with caution.

In 2006, when Jean White took her 'new look at psychoanalytic technique', she was able to conclude that although analysis remained deeply serious, for the Independent School in London at least it no longer required a 'po-faced attitude'. The therapist's laughter could be 'an interpretive action' – 'both a swift means of conveying understanding and a form of analytic management'. (And indeed elsewhere Adam Phillips has called getting a joke the model of a good interpretation.) 'Surprise in many forms', says White, 'a good joke or even a pointed piece of fun or mischief, the introduction of an unexpected perspective, even a piece of provocation or sarcasm ... can all keep the process alive and both parties moving on.' For those in acute or prolonged states of dis-ease with themselves, she reckoned, the Independent approach would feel reliable, predictable and safe. But those who felt ready to risk a more adventurous exploration of their inner world might have an experience that was 'unpredictable, even sometimes heady, startling or fun'.[6]

So humour may find a place in the consulting room as an 'interpretive action' or a tool of 'analytic management'. But is there something missing here, even a banana skin in waiting? Psychotherapists of different persuasions are hardly the first to think of 'using' humour to further their ends. As Chapter 7 explores, from earliest times people have tried to master and tame its spirit. But very often they discover that this is simply impossible. In its nature, humour is anarchic, unpredictable; it upends expectations and is finally no more biddable than quicksilver; as a form of communication, it is notoriously unreliable. In the end, it's often humour which uses us, not the other way round. Perhaps the best we can do is try to live good-humouredly with that.

But how good-humoured psychotherapy itself can be is another question. Since its beginnings, it has had a sense of itself as marginal, counter-cultural and misunderstood. Even now, when its practitioners are so numerous and its tenets have seeped their way into so many broader understandings, there is perhaps bound to be a misfit between the extraverted mainstream of Western societies, with their emphasis on measurable goals and achievements, and the introverted and diffuse search for meaning and inner purpose which may lead people to value radically other ways. The search may hardly seem very humorous, either, impelled as it may be by pain. So humour may have a hard time getting into this chapter. There are too many perceptual, institutional and even political barriers in its way.

These have crept up on it. For the first half of the twentieth century, people who were preoccupied with ideas of 'the unconscious' and worked as depth psychologists were pretty much seen as eccentrics. Even if their notions might seem threatening to prevailing social mores, they were hardly revolutionaries; those who consulted them were on the whole drawn from a socially narrow, relatively wealthy group whose inclination was for introverted self-exploration and whose interest lay in maintaining the lifestyle that supported it. But since the Second World War, the ideas of depth psychology have increasingly informed a collective Western notion of a well-being that is not just attainable but a general due. Once the idea of an unconscious that can be worked with has taken hold, it can hardly be ignored. Even if people feel they are not suffering more than they can manage after being involved in a tragic or terrifying event, *unconsciously they may be*. In a sense, we all live now with a perpetual psychological caveat: things may never be as they seem and at any time of personal or collective distress we may need especially trained others to interpret us to ourselves. This radical uncertainty has become part of the culture.

The huge expansion of psychotherapists is one evidence of that, and though not all of them will be influenced by ideas of the unconscious, a great number will. In the United States, Jeffrey Kottler reckons, the field is unrecognisable from what it was only 25 years ago. Then, clients were mostly white, female, middle class and drawn from among the 'worried well'; now they may come from any imaginable cultural or socioeconomic group and what ails them may be as diverse.[7] In Britain, psychotherapy organisations have burgeoned: there were well over 80 of them by 2014, their graduates also drawing clients in the widest of nets. But on both sides of the Atlantic, this very expansion of psychotherapy has also brought its opposite. Paradoxically, as expectations of where it may be helpful have increased, so funding and regulatory bodies have become more interested, limiting it and controlling what it offers.

Insurance companies used to pay without question for lengthy, intensive therapy for the few, says Kottler; now 'long-term therapy' is measured in months if not weeks. Publicly funded agencies offer 'managed care', which limits not only the time available but the sort of work that's allowed. As he sums it up: 'Everything is now about accountability, empirically supported evidence-based treatments, and measured outcomes, all within specific time parameters.' In Britain, the National Health Service's treatment of choice for mental distress is not psychodynamic psychotherapy, but short-term, outcome-oriented Cognitive Behavioural Therapy. It begins to look as if we can no longer afford the unconscious. 'Psychoanalysis today', laments Peter Fonagy, professor of that subject at University College London,

> is an embattled discipline. What hope is there in the era of empirically-validated treatments, which prize brief structured interventions, for a therapeutic approach which defines itself by freedom from constraint and preconception and counts treatment length not in terms of number of sessions but in terms of years?[8]

The same might be said for the many other analytically-based approaches on offer.

Many depth psychologists, for whom the unconscious is meat and drink, are ill-equipped to deal with such political realities. They are mostly introverts, observers rather than doers. They are more taken up with the complexities of inner worlds than happenings in outer ones; their expertise is in the minutiae of one-to-one relationships rather than the broad brush of societal ones. The fact that both they and their patients are inevitably embedded in and affected by a variety of cultural experience, for instance, has been curiously neglected in theoretical studies until relatively recently. This is true even among Jungians, whose ideas about a 'collective unconscious' might be thought to encourage them to be quite interested in what's going on around them. But it wasn't until 2004 that Singer and Kimbles brought out the first collection of Jungian papers on 'the cultural complex' in the collective psyche. In fact, many depth psychologists may share a tinge of the disdain towards the mundane world that Kenneth Eisold has observed among psychoanalysts. He knows what he is talking about, being himself both a psychoanalyst and an expert in the psychodynamics of organisations, and his critique is fairly stern:

> There is a certain privileged sense of immunity they feel from the ambition, envy, competition and turbulence of the world. Collectively, they tend to exempt themselves from scrutiny and judgement, justifying authoritarian and secretive policies by virtue of their deeper insights or greater responsibility; on the other hand, they feel victimised by those same practices.

This hauteur, he reckons, is written into the psychoanalytic project, going right back to Freud's own somewhat grandiose sense of heroic isolation. 'I was completely isolated in Vienna, I was shunned', he wrote of his early years, and then, 'In Europe, I felt as though I was despised.' But that was the destiny of one who had 'disturbed the sleep of the world': 'to stir up contradiction and arouse bitterness is the inevitable fate of psychoanalysis'.[9]

Psychoanalysts would not be the only ones to disparage a world that they feel misunderstands them. Others may also take pride in what Peter Lomas so memorably called 'the retreat from the ordinary', as they weave their theoretical complexities about what makes people tick. But disparagement and misunderstanding tend to feed on each other and bolster both. The long and tangled history of relationships between depth psychology and successive governments in Britain is one illustration of how much energy this can consume, and to how little psychotherapy and the wider world may still understand each other.

In Britain, depth psychologists like to think of themselves as members of a 'profession' and to claim traditional professional privileges: the self-validation of training programmes and qualifications for membership, the setting of their own standards of behaviour and practice, and the right to discipline those who contravene them. But there are two rather large drawbacks to this aspiration. The first is that these days the claims of professional privilege are generally seen with a critical if not suspicious eye, as doctors and lawyers well know. And the second is that psychotherapists collectively continue to fail one of the cardinal tests of a professional group. Far from basing their claims on a consistent body of knowledge, with coherent aims and predictable outcomes by which the individual whim of practitioners is disciplined, what they show each other and the world is a plethora of often incompatible, sometimes bitterly competing, theories and practices. There are still depth psychologists who aspire for recognition of their work as a 'science' rather than a form of art, and there may be more of them in future as they can draw more reliably on neuroscientific discoveries to back their theories. But trying to get the different groupings and schools to agree on a systematic body of knowledge, let alone one which can stand up to empirical standards of testing, makes trying to herd cats look simple.

So successive attempts to bring psychotherapy under statutory regulation have foundered: it has simply proved impossible over the years to get the different bodies to agree among themselves about what might be regulated and how. The first official enquiry in Britain reported as far back as 1971. This was actually occasioned by the activities of the Church of Scientology, but as its founder had claimed it to be 'the first thoroughly validated psychotherapy', Sir John Foster thought it well to have a closer look at the field more generally. He recommended that psychotherapy

> should be organised as a restricted profession open only to those who undergo an appropriate training and are willing to adhere to a ... proper code of ethics, and that the necessary legislation should be drafted and presented to Parliament as soon as possible.

Four years later, the Department of Health set up a working party to look at statutory registration, whose members included psychoanalysts and Jungian analysts, group analysts and psychiatrists. They agreed that statutory registration would be a good idea. But the British Association for Behavioural Psychotherapy, the only participating group whose members could claim a measurable effectiveness for their practice, put a rather definitive spoke in the wheels.

> There is no general agreement as yet on what constitutes a valid psychotherapeutic training, nor is there good evidence that patients benefit from treatment by most qualified psychotherapists. That some professional groups approve training courses is of little help to the public until it has been shown that the psychotherapy which is the subject of such courses in fact benefits patients.[10]

Forty years on, a great deal has changed. The training and ethical practice of psychotherapists is now overseen by different professional umbrella bodies, mostly in turn registered voluntarily with the official body which also, for instance, oversees the workings of the General Medical Council. For now at least, it looks as if depth psychologists have got what they have always wanted: officially recognised, self-regulating, professional status as well as 'official' recognition. But what the British Association for Behavioural Psychotherapy said all those years ago could still be claimed today.

So the rivalries, fallings out and antagonisms between different psychological groupings continue. What constitutes 'the unconscious' inevitably remains as hypothetical as ever, each version of it as valid or invalid as the next; the one we choose to work by is still the one that best suits our temperament rather than the one that's definitively 'true'. But this radical uncertainty continues to conjure the very opposite of good-humoured tolerance. It is as if the incompatibilities between Freud and Jung, their irrevocable theoretical falling-out embittered by their sense of personal betrayal, still haunts the psychological world they did so much to invent. Splitting, it seems, is what depth psychologists do, as fundamentalists retrench and conciliators approach and eclectics set up their own versions of 'the truth'. An endeavour dedicated to bringing the disparate elements of their individual patients into greater harmony seems to be caught in the very opposite when it comes to its collective life, as its institutions break apart, reform and break apart again. Even in the relatively small Jungian world this is so, with five separate 'Jungian' trainings in London alone, and half the Jungian societies in the world formed by splits and disagreements. These days too, Jungian analytical psychologists blur the time-honoured distinction between themselves and Freudians by increasingly calling themselves 'Jungian psychoanalysts'. This sort of thing could be accepted with good humour, even rejoiced over as a sign of creativity; the regroupings could be seen as much a sign of healthy diversity as is benign cell division at the biological end of human experience. Most often, however, it is lamented as destructive and damaging, painful to both individuals and institutions. And yet still it goes on.

Psychotherapy organisations have been likened to family firms, struggling to carry the energy of charismatic founders, caught in the toils of intergenerational and sibling rivalries. Olya Khaleelee's analogy is hardly cheerful, for the likelihood of such firms surviving into the third generation currently runs at about one in three; the odds may be further shortened by the insistence on turning out a product (more and more trainees) for whose wares the market is probably shrinking (see above). The very nature of the job, its essential emphasis on an intensity of one-to one relationships, is perhaps bound to make any sort of institutional life problematic. The main energy in psychotherapy organisations is engendered by a series of pairings: analysts and their trainees, supervisors and theirs. Each has their own loyalties, each wants their own to succeed. Kenneth Eisold sees the rigidity of psychoanalytic institutes as attempts to counter these potentially divisive pairings; this then, he suggests, sets up resentments which are projected on to the despised 'others' who profess a different approach or creed. The whole enterprise seems caught in an archetypal current of energies, now coming together, now splitting apart, its players buffeted first this way and then that.

In the end, and whatever the attempts at regulation, what therapists do in the privacy of their consulting rooms is between them and their patients and clients, and this is as least as much an expression of their own nature as of any creed. So what kind of people psychotherapists are does rather matter. At the end of her own sojourn among the psychoanalysts, Janet Malcolm likened them to so many eternal children, locked into a painful but protected world of unresolved parent–child transference. 'The people who instruct others on serious and final things themselves remain Peter Pans', she concluded, 'infinitely staving off adulthood and extinction in the Never-Never land of analytic practice and institutional politics.'[11]

There is, however, one big difference. Peter Pan's shadow was detachable. Psychotherapists must constantly be only too painfully aware of their own, whether outside the consulting room or within.

Notes

1. Kubie in Strean 101; Strean xii.
2. Strean xi.
3. Ibid.
4. Pierce in Strean 109.
5. Malcolm 53.
6. White 162, 165, 166; Phillips, *Freely Associated* 133.
7. Kottler vii–viii.
8. Ibid. viii; Fonagy 1.
9. Eisold 793; Freud in Eisold 793–794.
10. Foster in Shepherd 1558; British Association for Behavioural Psychotherapy in Shepherd.
11. Malcolm 155.

Chapter 5

Looking inwards

There's one thing that everybody thinks they know about psychotherapists, and by extension psychiatrists and other *mind* people too. And that is that they are at least as disturbed as those they treat. From Siri Hustvedt's psychoanalyst Erik Davidsen at one end of the literary canon, to Nicci French's psychotherapist turned sleuth Frieda Klein at the other, these are troubled souls. Sometimes they and their patients are figures of fun: think of all those delightfully mocking *New Yorker* cartoons. But ever since the first movies turned, the mind-doctors who've escaped from behind those high asylum walls and into our heads have been something else again. Occasionally they're helpful, but more often they're to be urgently avoided if we value our own sanity and even our life. Wasn't Hannibal Lector a brilliant psychiatric diagnostician?

Two heroic American researchers, John Flowers and Paul Frizler, once sat through more than 1,500 movies which featured psychotherapists, most broadly defined. Their project spanned the twentieth century, and they took in classics like *Spellbound* and *One Flew over the Cuckoo's Nest*, horrors like *Bloodsucking Pharaohs in Pittsburgh*, and everything before, after and in between. Only in the aftermath of the Second World War, when it seemed that traumatised troops might benefit from the knowledge and skills of European psychoanalytic refugees, did they find that the mind-doctors came out well. Overall, in 80 per cent of the movies, they appeared unethical, incompetent or just plain bad.

This sort of thing is perhaps bound to have its effect.

'And what do you do?'
'I'm a psychotherapist, a Jungian analyst.'
'Oh. Well, I'd better watch what I say then!'

There can't be many of us who haven't met this response, jocular but maybe not entirely. Perhaps those jokes about the mad-doctors have something self-protective in them, a precautionary deflection of the possibility that we really can read into minds, understand something about other people that they don't know themselves. The fact that we're ethically debarred from talking about our work doesn't help dispel the uneasy mystique (and probably means that we spend too much time with each other as well). 'Alienists' is what the mind-doctors used to be called, and alien we still to an extent remain. We may be imbued with the healer's power, and most people are ambivalent about the enormity of that. We rail against the arrogance of doctors who 'never tell us anything' – and at the same time just want them to get on with being the grownups here; we long for them to make it better and fear that they can't or even won't.

'Doctor, doctor, I don't seem to be able to get up in the morning. It takes me half an hour to find the energy to face the day.'
'Well, get up half an hour later, then.'

'Doctor, doctor, that hurts!'
'Right, I'll try a blunter knife.'

The ambivalence is an ancient one: these chestnuts were probably already old when they appeared in an ancient Roman joke-book.[1]

Yet the jokes about psychotherapists who are more neurotic, less able to deal with real life than their patients, may contain some grains of truth. There can't be many other careers where personal experience of psychological distress is a positive recommendation. But this is one of them, for this is what enables people to stand empathically alongside the sufferings of others. Nina Coltart pinpointed the paradox succinctly: 'Psychotherapists are trained from their weaknesses; all other professions build on their strengths.' Therapists may recognise this with a certain stoic pride, evoking the Wounded Healer as patron. This image appears across time and culture. It is personified in Chiron, the incurably wounded ancient Greek centaur who taught his craft to Asclepius, the god of healing; it is carried through the widespread tales of shamans, who endure the agonising journey to upper and lower worlds to bring healing to their people; it has lasting life in the story of Jesus Christ himself. The transformations of suffering brought by these healers are also psychotherapy's purpose; their stories bring hope to its patients and often its practitioners too. There's a seductive danger here, as Jungian analyst Sidney Handel has pointed out: psychotherapists need to beware of imagining that their own pain and suffering make them rather special. But even if they know their sufferings are in fact no greater than anyone else's, something in them seems to remain fascinated by not only their own troubled psychological states, but those of others as well.[2]

One of the other dinner-party remarks that often comes our way is 'I don't know how you do it.' The old alchemists, in whose labours Jung saw a metaphor for psychotherapy's own, called their solitary and taxing work an *opus contra naturam*, a work against nature. And so psychotherapy may also seem to be. Why would anyone want to spend a working life not just engaging with the sufferings of others but actually seeking these out, choosing to bear witness to such stories as could break your heart if you let them? These stories and their possible meanings make for often deep and rewarding bonds between therapists and their patients. Yet once the therapy is over, therapists seldom (and quite rightly) know what happened next. Rather like old-fashioned jobbing nannies, left with fading snapshots of those they once fostered with such care, we never know what became of people when they grew beyond us.

These and other sufferings are not so often written about. Psychotherapists are schooled in reticence: not talking about yourself or letting slip unconsidered reactions are considered cardinal rules of the therapeutic exchange. This may be changing, under the influence of the US-based school of 'relational analysis' and what neuroscientists are finding out about the roots and workings of emotion (see Chapter 11). Nevertheless, it's still generally believed that to go on to patients about how we sometimes find them trying or hurtful would hardly help them trust our professional capacities to bear their distress until they can do so for themselves; it might even confirm their worst dread about their own unacceptability. But that doesn't mean we aren't human beings too, bound to be affected by the continual companionship of suffering, the seepage of patients' anger and grief, and the weight of ambiguity and uncertainty that must accompany any work with unconscious worlds. I have long had the impression that more psychotherapists than you might expect become increasingly deaf in their later years. Perhaps this is why.

Marvin Speigelman, a Jungian analyst who also analysed many other therapists in his time, wrote eloquently of the possible costs of the endeavour. Above all, he thought, therapists are dogged by depression: in the very nature of their uncertain work, they must be 'specialists in the darkness of the soul', bound to experience more failures than physicians or lawyers as they reach for the unattainable goal of psychological wholeness. The work is bound to bring anxiety too, and a sense of powerlessness as they puzzle about what they are doing, what they should be doing and where it might lead. Psychotherapists are schooled to accept what comes their way; their behaviour is rightly constrained within strict ethical guidelines. They must check their own feelings of impatience, or retaliatory aggression, and this takes its toll. Psychotherapists are prey to deep muscular tensions, which sitting for hours on end in constant alertness to nuances of communication can only exacerbate. And what, really, are they and their efforts worth? Patients might not believe that questions around money and what fees represent are so vexed among therapists that the whole topic is hardly discussed. All these burdens, thought Spiegelman, go with the job. And to make them heavier yet, they can't be shared. The alienists are still alien to society's mainstream and even their attempts to find community among their own are hardly, as we've seen, a heart-warming success.[3]

All this said and more, however, Spiegelman would not have had it otherwise, for this was only one side of his story. For him, the image of the Wounded Healer seemed too dark altogether; it left out, he thought, the healing effects of joy and laughter, and the huge rewards of the work, which were as uplifting as the sufferings were burdensome. Not everyone will recognise their own therapeutic self in Spiegelman's heartfelt catalogue. Indeed, when invited to respond to it, Michael Fordham, the founder of the 'London School' of Jungian psychology, was bracing in his disavowal: 'I do not suffer much with my patients and many of my patients do not suffer much either, indeed if they can do so productively I think their analysis is drawing to a close.'[4] But for many, at least some of Spiegelman's sufferings, some of the time, may strike a chord. The question doesn't go away: why on earth do psychotherapists choose to do it?

Put simply, it suits the kind of people we by and large, and *pace* Fordham, are. Suffering is what we're drawn to, what we're curiously comfortable with, because we recognise it. In one way or another, we've been there ourselves. This doesn't only, as Nina Coltart said, give us a career advantage; choosing this path also helps us make sense of our own distress. Jung would probably have approved of this. He reckoned that a good half of any psychotherapy was about the therapist's self-examination, 'for only what he can put right in himself can he hope to put right in the patient ... it is his own hurt that gives the measure of his power to heal'.[5] Therapists try hard to be alert to the dangers of unconsciously using their trade for their own benefit rather than that of their patients. Kottler quotes one large American survey which found that mostly they were well aware of being in the job primarily to make sense of their own lives. (We might be more worried about another study, which found that their motivation was often unresolved or skirted over in their own therapeutic self-examination.)[6] But very many of us do know, for instance, that we've been attuned to other people's needs since early childhood, when tending to our parents' own distress seemed essential to keeping the safety of the home. This may give us a particular alertness to unspoken signals, and so a greater sensitivity to what's going on with our patients and clients. It may also, however, have left us with a lot of unmet needs of our own. So care-taking is not just what we are attuned to do, but a way to feel better about our own needs by tending them, as it were, at one remove. Psychotherapy may fill other emotional gaps as well. One reason at least for the overwhelming preponderance of middle-aged women among its practitioners – and one reason too why so many find a focus for their work in stories about early mother–infant relationships – may be that the consulting room welcomes maternal instincts which are looking for a home.

This may begin to sound quite a cosy fit. But of course cosy it isn't. Psychotherapists are not friends or mothers or (certainly not) lovers to their patients, much as one or both sides may sometimes wish they were. A huge part of the theoretical justification of what psychotherapy does and why it may work is based on this very clash between desire and reality. For Aaron Green, this was the worst part of his work: not in the end the inescapable Oedipal rivalries of the Institute, but 'this chronic struggle to keep oneself from doing the things that decent people naturally and spontaneously do'.[7] The demands of this analytic abstinence can be extraordinarily detailed – and keenly debated too. The shape, purpose and abuse of therapeutic boundaries is surely one of the hottest, and sometimes most painful, topics among psychotherapists and often their patients as well. How many acres of professional print have been expended on when, if ever, it's justifiable for therapists to say something about themselves? But it doesn't end there. Some practitioners, for instance, may be quite exercised about whether to greet a patient with a smile, or when it may be justifiable to pass the Kleenex or put a comforting hand on a shoulder, or whether to interpret, or even accept, the small bunch of flowers that a patient brings. Not all therapists are so engrossed in the labyrinthine ways of therapeutic transference. Classical Jungians, for instance, are more inclined to believe that the therapeutic relationship is contained in a psyche that goes way beyond the two individuals involved. They at least may not be surprised to hear that humour seems to want its own say here (see particularly Chapter 11).

The abstinences of the psychotherapist may for some people, some of the time, compound the difficulties of the job. Yet they may also help make it attractive to people who long to find satisfaction in deepening relationships but want to keep these as far as they can under their own control. People who remember their own childhood as insecure or worse are likely to have a hard time trusting close relationships, and the consulting room may offer them the chance to build a safe haven for themselves as well as their patients. A relationship set within boundaries of time and place, with a repertoire of acceptable responses defined by custom and ethical codification, might suit them well. Not all psychotherapists by any means ask their patients to lie on a couch, while they seat themselves out of direct vision. But many do, especially those most influenced by the conventions of psychoanalysis. The original idea for this 'certain ceremonial' was Freud's, and his reasons for it were not unmixed. Some were technical: he didn't want the changing expressions on his face, as he gave himself over to 'the current of his unconscious thoughts', to influence what his patients thought or told him; he wanted their transference to him to be clearly expressed, uncontaminated by associations. But first of all his motive was personal: 'I cannot put up with being stared at by other people for eight hours a day (or more).'[8]

Psychotherapeutic theory and technique may seem 'objective'. But here is a perfect illustration of how both are inevitably intertwined with the subjectivity of each practitioner and theory. This is as true now as it was at the start, so it's no wonder that a definitive 'version' of psychotherapy is so elusive. From their theory, Jungians might seem likely to bring a more optimistic, even more humorous attitude to life and so to their work than their Freudian counterparts. Jung himself certainly found the keynote of Freud's thought, in contrast to his own, to be 'devastatingly pessimistic'. For him, Freud remained a physician, always focused on the clinical picture of the neurosis that was causing his patients grief.

> Anyone who has this picture before him always sees the flaw in everything, and ... must always point out ... the weak spot, the unadmitted wish, the hidden resentment, the secret, illegitimate fulfilment of a wish distorted by the censor.

Like the dentist, Freud must ever be focused on drilling out the caries, and in the most painful way. But where, Jung wondered, was the gold filling? His own focus was very different. His essential belief in psyche's purpose, and even desire, for humans to become more conscious of their true natures, led him to see neurotic symptoms not as sickness but as attempts to redress psychological imbalance; neurosis arose when people lost a sense of meaning in their lives. And for him, the quest for 'individuation', painful though it might sometimes be, was also a way of wonder, for beneath the repressed pain of each individual unconscious there lay the vast wealth of the collective realm of human possibility, for good as well as ill. If Freud focused on drilling out the caries in the personal unconscious, Jung's bent was to follow the old alchemists in their search for the pure gold of psyche itself. For him, the model of the psychotherapist was not the physician but the philosopher. His entire work, he said at the end of his long life, had been 'fundamentally nothing but attempts, ever renewed, to give an answer to the question of the interplay between the "here" and the "hereafter"'.[9]

Jung may hardly be the most reliable guide to the essence of Freud's thought; this summation, from his obituary of his old mentor-turned-rival, carries a weight of unassuaged bitterness. To paint Jung's followers as naturally more cheerfully optimistic, more seized by delight in exploring human complexities than Freud's, would be too easy altogether. These days too, the differences between the two approaches are increasingly blurred, as 'Jungian psychoanalysts' lie their patients on the couch in search of transference rather than following Jung's insistence on the face to face encounter of two human souls in a mutual search for meaning. But in the end, there are still two radically different understandings of the nature of the human being behind the theories and techniques. 'Homo homini lupus', said Freud. 'Man is a wolf to man. Who in the face of all his experience of life and of history will have the courage to dispute this assertion?' But we are also much more than that, and the Jungian way lies in the never-ending attempt to uncover and reconcile our infinite opposites. On this path, there is more enlivening delight in amplifying the understanding of dreams through exploration of myths, fairy tales and the wealth of historical beliefs than there ever could be in Freud's view of the dream as one more neurotic symptom, a disguised fulfilment of a repressed wish. It says something perhaps about the contemporary worldview that it is Freud's approach rather than Jung's that has so prevailed. But for those who see things differently, the burgeoning of psychotherapy is more than a dour attempt to reconcile ourselves to conflict both outside and within. For them, it carries a search for greater psychological wholeness, and with that, as the American analyst John Beebe says, a recognition of 'the *profound pleasure* that the discovery of integrity brings' (my italics).[10]

Well, I would say that, wouldn't I? But I'm certainly not the only one to wonder whether there isn't too much negative emphasis altogether in psychotherapy's prevailing preoccupations and approaches. Herbert Strean clearly thought so, and he did a 'computer search' of some of the major characteristics of psychoanalysis and other psychotherapeutic approaches to underline his thesis. He found nearly 600 entries under 'hate', 'hostility' and 'rage'. And under laughter and humour? Thirty-eight. Twenty years later, in 2014, many more such straws could be plucked from the world wide wind. The online archive of the *International Journal of Psychoanalysis* yielded 113 references to humour, 421 to mourning, 326 to hatred and 753 to loss. In the *Journal of Analytical Psychology*, the main international Jungian publication, comparable figures were 92, 214, 154 and 472. The *British Journal of Psychotherapy* came up with 112, 320, 268 and 132.

These numbers games may at least lead us to wonder about psychotherapists' apparent preoccupations, and what sort of worldview they offer their patients. They may not do so directly, and they may start from an assumption that the relationship between the two of them is in any case largely based on the illusions of 'transference'. Nevertheless, there are two 'real' people in the room as well, and the very nature of their relationship makes both of them extremely alert to what may be going on in the other, whether voiced or not. As the British Jungian Warren Colman has pointed out, it's well known that analysts can't help but reveal their own values. He gives a nice instance of that from a sharp-witted patient across the Atlantic: this man knew his analyst's political loyalties, because every time he criticised the Democrats, the analyst interpreted it, and every time he said anything positive about them, it passed without comment.[11]

We don't know whether the man was swayed to vote Democrat himself. But such is the nature of the therapeutic relationship that people find the views of their therapist enormously influential. So the therapist's beliefs about the way of the world must matter a great deal. If they see the human condition as primarily one of loss, mourning and hatred, then these may well be what they encourage their patients to dwell on. At the limit, the very therapy they offer may confirm the inevitability of the suffering that brought their patients to them in the first place. One of Herbert Strean's contributors, the psychoanalyst Michael Bader, showed just how powerfully this might play out when personal characteristics dovetail with theory and technique. The idea of the analyst as unresponsive, rigid and humourless was, he found, a caricature. But all the same, he found it true that some of those drawn to the work will 'tend to have inhibitions about the spontaneous expression of feeling, including passion and humor, as well as a certain propensity for depression'. These characteristics are probably, he reckoned, no greater than in the general population. But there's a difference: these are characteristics which psychoanalytic theory and technique may not only justify but also reinforce. So patients may be offered not a way towards healing of their painful story, but an action replay: the therapist's 'neutrality' and 'abstinence' may echo their parents' emotional absence and rejection. Both parties are reinforced in an understanding of the world which brought them together in the first place. As the British analyst Adam Phillips has so memorably put it: 'The risk for someone going to see a psychoanalyst is that one dispiriting story will meet another even more dispiriting one.'[12]

If this glum picture were the only one, then the whole psychotherapeutic enterprise would be incomprehensible indeed except as a work of profound mutual melancholy. For some, this may indeed be so. For others, there will also be melancholy in the acceptance that they will never have the ideal past for which they have craved. But countless therapists and their patients could also attest to the pleasure, enjoyment and sometimes exhilaration to be had as they discover a more ample and kindlier sense of themselves and their world's creative possibilities. It is hard to think where that discovery is to begin for someone in a greater distress than they alone can currently bear, except in the therapist's own attitudes and expectations. Yet still this may not be emphasised. Nina Coltart was one who set great store by enjoyment of the work; she felt that if therapists were predominantly worried and anxious about it, then somehow they were on the wrong wavelength. But the title of her deservedly still-selling primer on the therapeutic art hardly conveys that message. *How to Survive as a Psychotherapist* must irrevocably conjure images of teeth-gritted endurance at the least, and the threat of agonising extinction at worst. The text emphasises often enough that 'survival-with-enjoyment' is what the author means. But someone must once have thought that survival-without-it answered more to the expectations of potential readerships among therapists and their clientele. The notion is reinforced to this day, each time the book's title is displayed.

The idea of analysis as more grim than enjoyable is one that Christopher Bollas took on when he pinpointed a 'worrying exclusion' from the psychoanalytic literature. This he called 'the analyst's celebration of the analysand': of their instincts for life and love, their creativity and admirable accomplishments both inside and beyond the consulting room. In his exploration of analytic celebration, perhaps the most telling aspect is his take on why it should have been so ignored. From the start, he assumes that it is harder to analyse the patient's instincts for life than their urges for destruction, that one of the most difficult things to talk about in an analysis is the mutual pleasure the work may bring. Why should it be, he wonders, that analysts often feel on surer ground when they can detect pervasive negative transference and dismiss the positive as no more than 'defensive idealisation'? Perhaps, he muses, they need to oppose their patients, or to advertise to colleagues just how clever they are at understanding what's really going on, how unflinchingly they have analysed the negative feelings that the patient unconsciously harbours towards them.

Here's a Bollas attitude test. A patient mocks him, thinking up scenarios which put him on the spot, and go quite beyond his interpretive capacity. And Bollas laughs, not just because these are actually very funny, but because he finds in them cause for celebration of the patient's growing sense of his own self, of his right to exist and his capacity to relate. But this would not, says Bollas, be the reaction of some colleagues. He finds it painful to say it, but he surmises that they would see this mockery as nothing but a sign of negative transference, motivated by envy. Colleagues might think the same (though Bollas doesn't specifically say so) of his celebration of his patients' aggression, his explicit reassurance that they have a right to have a go at him and his interpretations.[13]

'I wonder', the influential analyst Wilfred Bion once asked,

> if it is within the rules of psychoanalysis to laugh at ourselves? Is it according to the rules of psychoanalysis that we should be amused and find things funny? Is it permissible to enjoy a psychoanalytic meeting? I suggest that, having broken through in this revolutionary matter of being amused in the sacred process of psychoanalysis, we might as well continue to see where that more joyous state of mind might take us.[14]

Notes

1 Bremmer 17.
2 Coltart, *Survive* 39; Handel xiii.
3 Spiegelman 127–148.
4 Fordham in Spiegelman 148.
5 Jung, 'Fundamental Questions' 16:239.
6 Kottler 2.
7 Malcolm 77.
8 Freud, 'On Beginning the Treatment' X11:133–134.
9 Jung, 'In Memory of Sigmund Freud' 15:60–73; Jung, *Memories* 330.
10 Freud, 'Civilisation' XXI:111; Beebe 19.
11 Colman, 'Reflections' 210.
12 Bader in Strean 44; Phillips 'I Feel Guilty' 14–15.
13 Bollas, *Forces* 77–92.
14 Bion quoted in Coltart, *Slouching* 11.

What's so funny?

Chapter 6

Senses of humour

So what was Iambe's joke, its effects so powerful that it brought solace to individual tragedy and turned the threat of global extinction towards a renewal of life? It seems entirely fitting that Homer gives us no clue about this, and that no one yet knows the answer for sure. What is it that makes any of us grin or guffaw, or smile, or smirk? What cheers us up and restores, however momentarily, our good humour? The answers are so individual and so culturally varied that they tell us more about ourselves than about anything more universal. This is reason enough perhaps for psychotherapists to find humour interesting. But it also makes it extraordinarily difficult to pin down and explain, as slippery as Mercury himself.

Maybe this is why the topic remains so enticing. Theories about humour's nature have multiplied since antiquity. By the time that Cicero, the most renowned of Roman orators, wrote his treatise on that art in the mid-50s BCE, there was already a bevy of 'self-proclaimed experts' on laughter's origins and actions. He – a notorious jokester himself – saw no shame in his own failure to understand these, because the experts didn't either.[1] Plenty of people have tried since then. But once the idea of an autonomous unconscious mind took hold, there were further reasons for bafflement. 'Strictly speaking', said Freud in his own major exploration of jokes and the unconscious, 'we do not know what we are laughing at.' The point seemed so important to him that in all the early editions the sentence was italicised.[2]

That said, Freud did of course have his own theory, which answered another question. Why do people still laugh at 'quite wretched' jokes, particularly obscene ones? His answer lay in the purpose of the joke rather than its 'technique'. The pleasure felt came from a release of the psychic energy that had until then been used in keeping an inadmissible thought or feeling out of consciousness. Unsurprisingly perhaps, these were mostly to do with sexuality or hostility. The ways in which Freud thought jokes worked – through condensation, displacement, representation by the opposite – also tallied nicely with his ideas on the workings of dreams, about which he had published his major work five years earlier.

Freud's 1905 study was not his last word on humour. More than two decades later, he wrote a short paper which fitted it with his then current thinking about the relationship between ego and superego. There will be more on this in the next chapter. But for now, it seems worth noting that Freud's changing views of humour illustrate a wider point: any theory of humour will depend on the overall notions the author has at the time about the nature of the human being. 'When it comes to what amuses us', says the philosopher Simon Critchley in his extraordinarily quotable book *On Humour*, 'we are all authorities, experts in the field.' (So the very audacity or arrogance of trying to write a philosophy of humour, he adds, might actually be a sort of joke in itself, or at least a dramatic irony.)[3]

The intensely individual perception of what's funny has never, however, stopped theorists from trying to discern more general rules. Most writings focus on laughter, perhaps because it's the most obvious indication of being in good humour, being amused. But what they say can also be applied to other manifestations of humour too, from the smile ('little laugh' in many languages) to the smirk and beyond. These days, theorists focus on three main categories, of which the most recent is the nineteenth century 'relief theory', as exemplified by Freud. The next, first articulated a century earlier, has to do with incongruity: humour arises in the discrepancy between what we expect and what actually happens. One recent theorist, for instance, claims to have found just one truly universal joke: the lurching progress of a drunk is everywhere irresistible because of the discrepancies between their skewed perceptions and the audience's more sober grasp of reality.[4] (But even this may not work for everyone all the time. We could imagine for instance that it might be quite difficult for children of an alcoholic parent to join in the fun.)

The third main theory, perhaps the most disquieting to contemporary sensibilities, is also the oldest and most durable of all: we laugh at other people because we feel superior to them. We feel good because they feel bad. This idea goes back to Aristotle and Plato and has its best-known exponent in the seventeenth century English philosopher Thomas Hobbes. Laughter, as he famously said, was nothing else but 'a sudden glory arising from sudden conception of some eminency in ourselves, by comparison with the infirmity of others'. Or, he added, 'with our own formerly': people enjoy the remembrance of their own follies as long as these are safely behind them. Elsewhere, he builds on this psychologically astute perception: the people who are most likely to feel this 'sudden glory' are those who are conscious of the fewest abilities in themselves, 'who are forced to keep themselves in their own favour, by observing the imperfections of other men'.[5]

These three main theories – superiority, incongruity and relief – may be useful catchalls, but their boundaries are hardly watertight. Aristotle appreciated the incongruous as well as the lure of superiority. ('On he came, his feet shod with his ... chilblains' is one of his.)[6] Modern theories are no easier to corral. To take one instance: Henri Bergson, the highly influential French philosopher whose book on laughter came out in the same year as Freud's on dreams, thought that we laugh when we see people acting like machines, rigid and repetitive in their movements rather than fluently adapting to their actual environment. If we laugh at a pompously prosperous businessman suddenly taking a tumble on a banana skin, we can perhaps see why Bergson's theory has been claimed for both superiority and incongruity. And once more, the theory needs to be put into the theoriser's context. Bergson proposed that humans were animated by an *élan vital*, a general libido that fuelled both evolution and creativity; it was when this force was interrupted that actions became mechanical, and laughter was a necessary prompt to get the flow going again.

Individual theorists live in their own times and societies too. For Simon Critchley, Bergson's theory really comes alive when he thinks of the contemporary dawn of the cinema, of the jerky person-becomes-thing movements of the great silent comedians. For me, Hobbes' views about what makes people laugh are entirely consistent with his belief that the primary human motivation was a 'perpetual and restless desire for power', a potential if not actual war of all against all, which notoriously rendered human life 'solitary, poor, nasty, brutish and short'. This bleak assessment is perhaps understandable when we remember that he was writing at a time of acute political tension that erupted into the particular agonies of a civil war.[7]

So what we find funny is intensely personal, related to our overall view of life, and coloured by our cultural and social experience. These are all reasons why senses of humour can yield valuable psychological insights into who we are, a dig in the ribs to point us towards the questions about individual identity which are the basic stuff of consulting room encounters. Perhaps they are also reasons for psychotherapists schooled against self-revelation to be wary of letting their clients see too much of what makes them guffaw or grin, or smirk or smile.

There may be other reasons to be wary too. Surprise is humour's essence. It can't be planned for, bypassing every effort to corral it into 'technique'. First the laugh, then the intellectual effort to find out why it came: if humour is to work at all, that must be the rule. Even where enjoyment is tinged with pleasurable expectation born of past experience, the actual moment of denouement has to be unpredictable. The old jokes may be the best – but not if the audience knows the punch line in advance. 'Look behind you!' we shout again at the hapless about-to-be-victim of the pantomime trickster or villain. We know they'll never turn in time. But exactly how and when they come to grief must always be a surprise if it's to raise a laugh at all.

Humour can be an uninvited guest, turning up when we least expect it. In antiquity, that's what entertainers often did, gatecrashing a dinner party in the hope of a meal in return for raising a laugh. Even when ritualised, codified and 'professionalised', humour remains edgy; it still comes *from somewhere else*, now as in antiquity. Aristotle wrote in his *Poetics* about comedians who wandered from village to village, excluded contemptuously from Athens. It took centuries for the travelling troupes of buffoons and jokers, and their descendants in the Italian *commedia del arte*, and their descendants again in the stock figures of British pantomime, to find a permanent theatrical home. Most of the 'alternative' comedians he's met, says one commentator, are 'misfits'.[8] 'The joker in the pack' is what we call the unexpected, the disrupter of established assumptions. 'The fool in Tarot goes everywhere' was the old saying; the joker still is the only card in the deck without a number. Humour has no place in the hierarchy, but it can get in everywhere. And its ways may be devious too. The English word 'smile' is directly related to the Danish *smila*. But another dictionary definition takes it back to Old English *smuzan*, 'to creep'.

In the sometimes delightfully revealing, often challenging, always edgy relationships between humour and the established order, the city and the outsider, it's not hard to find analogies with the interplay between ego and unconscious. Psychotherapists know well how a sudden, unexpected meeting of the two can enliven, enlighten and even transform, bringing a re-cognition of something that is both quite new and profoundly familiar. These moments have been described in many different ways, from the glorious simplicity of a sudden 'Aha!' to the complexity of a Jungian 'experience of the Self'. Christopher Bollas writes of a recognition of the 'unthought known', Donald Kalsched of a shared glimpse of a 'soul-full mystery at the heart of personality'. Catherine Crowther and Martin Schmidt, both London Jungians, write eloquently of these 'states of grace', or 'Eureka moments': something is received, often by both analyst and client in an extraordinary synchronicity, that comes from beyond the ego's thought and transforms the feeling tone and the relationship. 'We both burst into laughter in a shared moment of delighted surprise', writes Catherine Crowther of one such experience.[9]

Laughter can be a response to a state of grace. But it may be a state of grace in itself as well. Like grace, laughter eludes rational or causal explanation: these can only come in its echo. The Latin 'gratia' brings us to grace as something that imparts beauty, and to gratitude. The Biblical Greek 'charis' can be seen as the operation of God's purpose in the human heart – which finds, as Martin Schmidt points out, a secular expression in Jung's concept of individuation as the continual movement towards a great human wholeness. To be able to laugh with sheer and joyful delight at sudden intimations of that movement, with a sense of gratitude that goes beyond cause or intent, is surely one of the greatest gifts of being human.

There seems to be little celebration of this in the many philosophical puzzlings over what laughter and humour are about. But in the final paragraph of his own work on jokes and the unconscious, Freud does perhaps touch on it. All the sources of pleasure that he's been elaborating, he says – all the economies of expenditure on inhibition, ideation and feeling – boil down to one thing: an attempt to return a time when psychic life demanded less expenditure of energy altogether. This is 'the mood of our childhood, when we were ignorant of the comic, when we were incapable of jokes and when we had no need of humour to make us feel happy in our life'.[10] Here's a 'state of grace' that goes beyond any need for theories to explain us to ourselves. It could even be likened to the 'dream of totality', that intimation of psychological unity, which Jung called the

Self. Perhaps one task of the psychotherapist is to help their clients keep that dream alive through the confusion and pain of their self-divisions?

Meanwhile, there's humour to help us live with those, and its methods may be tough indeed. 'Jokes tear holes in our usual predictions about the empirical world', begins Simon Critchley. 'The comic world is ... the world with its causal chains broken, its social practices turned inside out, and common sense rationality left in tatters.' Tearing, breaking, shredding: there is no escaping humour's inherent violence. Jokes are 'killing' and what kills is the *punch* line. In Britain, there's a contemporary lust for what used to be called 'alternative' stand-up comedy, now so widespread as to be mainstream. Its practitioners 'take on' their audiences, trading insults, knowing they can 'die a death' if they aren't 'slaying them', if they don't find the 24 carat gag, 'the stuff that kills'. Kill or be killed: 'Comedy all comes back to the banana skin', says the highly successful Jack Dee. 'We laugh because we're glad it hasn't happened to us.' The comedic may demand what Bergson called 'something like a momentary anaesthesia of the heart'. There is, says Critchley, a certain coldness at laughter's core.[11]

There is savagery in superiority, too, From antiquity onwards, humour has ridden most gleefully of all on the back of other people's inferiority or discomfort. Here's Tertullian, one of the founders of Western Christendom, warning against enjoyment of theatres, gymnastics and other shows. None of these pagan delights, he told his flock, could possibly rival the spectacle offered by the last and eternal Day of Judgement.

> What a panorama that will be! And watching it, what will strike me with wonder? What will make me laugh? I shall rejoice, I shall exult to see so many kings and emperors – who, we were told, would be taken up into heaven with Jove when they died – groaning in the deepest darkness along with those who foretold their heavenly glory.... There will be acrobats to watch, jumping about much more nimbly on account of the fire. There will be charioteers to gaze at, red all over in wheels of flame, and gymnasts to enjoy, flying through the air not in a fairground but in an inferno.
>
> And a great deal more besides.[12]

Tertullian's polemic may be extreme; caustic humour was his rhetorical weapon of choice. But his times were not gentle either. In Roman marketplaces, slaves with obvious physical or mental abnormalities could command high prices; there's at least one account of a dissatisfied customer who paid a good price for a cretin, only to demand his money back when he discovered the man had all his wits about him. Dwarfs enhanced dinner table entertainments, tumbling about or displayed naked and bejewelled – which certainly sounds safer than the alternative of being sent into the arena to do battle with each other, wild animals or 'Amazons'.[13] Impossible perhaps to tell from today's distance just what they represented for their owners and in their times. But surely their appearance and antics could be guaranteed to raise a good laugh, or they'd hardly be worth their keep.

And so dwarfs tumbled through the centuries, served up with the fruit to delight Catherine de Medici's serving ladies, privileged as court jesters, staples of the nineteenth century travelling freak show, objects of medical curiosity, until they finally found a society of their own in Munchkin Country in the 1939 movie of *The Wizard of Oz*. These were the lucky ones. Many more travelled the years with a motley collection of others whose appearance or behaviour cast them immediately as 'outsiders', putting on what show they could to earn a hard crust.

The very word Enlightenment, with all its associations of rationality, refinement and wit, suggests that by the eighteenth century their time was up. 'Humour', the French thought then, was a peculiarly English thing. In his *Encyclopaedia,* Diderot, or one of his Company of Men of Letters, described it as designating 'an original, uncommon and singular pleasantry'. And among the English, he wrote, this could have far more effect than the most serious and well-argued works, as Jonathan Swift's 'Modest Proposal' well showed. By suggesting that the English eat little Irish children with their cauliflowers, 'Swift was able to hold back the English government which was otherwise ready to remove the last means of sustenance and commerce from the Irish people.' The English word 'humour' has since found its way into the French language. The *Dictionnaire de l'Academie Française* has defined it as 'a form of irony, at once pleasant and serious, sentimental and satirical' peculiar to the English spirit, 'an entirely British disposition to be amused without bitterness by ridiculous, absurd or unusual aspects of reality'.[14]

This might have pleased Lord Chesterfield, the eighteenth century politician and man of letters. In one of his celebrated *Letters to His Son*, written from Bath – where else? – he counsels the young man most particularly on how to make a good impression on others. Reflect, urges Chesterfield, on how a slovenly figure, or an ungraceful manner of speech, prejudices you against another from the start – and on how the opposite is also true. The exact ingredients of that pleasing *je ne sais quoi* are, he says, indefinable. But it most certainly does not include laughing, and he most heartily wishes never to hear his son laugh for as long as he lives.

> Frequent and loud laughter is the characteristic of folly and ... the manner in which the mob express their silly joy at silly things; and they call it being merry.... True wit, or sense, never yet made anybody laugh; they are above it: They please the mind, and give cheerfulness to the countenance. But it is low buffoonery, or silly accidents, that always excite laughter, and that is what people of sense and breeding should show themselves above.

Chesterfield thought himself neither melancholy nor cynical, and as apt to be pleased as anybody. But 'I am sure that, since I have had the full use of my reason, nobody has ever heard me laugh.'[15]

Plenty of others of his sort and time, however, had no such sentiments. And as one study of more than 200 eighteenth century joke books shows plain as day, what they laughed at was the misery of others. These books were far too expensive for 'the mob', and very many of their jokes played unmercifully on people of 'sense and breeding' getting a rise out of their inferiors, and mocking their deformities. Here's a particular favourite: trick a poor, blind pie woman into crying her wares in church, when she thinks she's on a street corner. And did you hear the good 'frolick' about the two aristocrats and the old woman boiling apples at Charing Cross? They delight her with the promise of a bushel of charcoal, then stuff it with gunpowder. So the whole lot blows up, overturning her kettle and scattering her apples about her ears. Counsel sick old people to go hang themselves and see if that improves matters, kick away the cripple's crutches ('Can't put *you* straight!'), toss dwarfs into pigpens and lame matrons into a ditch. All good for a laugh. And here's another idea: summon a stable boy or kitchen maid to your elegant dinner table and ask them to translate a line of Virgil.[16]

The contrast between these ideas of a joke and 'Enlightenment values' could hardly be greater, and 'people of sense and breeding' increasingly found human deprivation and wretchedness a focus for philanthropy rather than fun. After 1770 London's Bedlam hospital no longer offered its lunatics as a visitor attraction for anyone who wanted a good laugh and had a penny or two to spare. (Another indication of the times: until then, while paying sightseers were welcome, doctors and clergy who wished to treat and comfort were forbidden to visit at all.) By the end of the nineteenth century, another sort of visitor attraction was beginning to rebel. In 1898, the members of a travelling troupe – no longer precariously freelance but money-spinners for the Barnam and Bailey Circus – called a protest meeting against their 'opprobrious' designation as 'Freaks'. Convened by the Bearded Lady, the meeting was chaired by the Human Adding Machine, and the Armless Wonder recorded the minutes with his feet. The meeting appealed to the public for an alternative designation, and rejected 300 possibilities before agreeing on 'prodigies', suggested by the Bishop of Winchester. The name never caught on in America, and there's a suspicion that the whole thing may have been dreamed up by the Barnum and Bailey PR people as publicity for the show.[17]

And the show still goes on. In 1933, Robert Ripley, already famous for his Believe It Or Not cartoons, opened his first Odditorium at the Chicago World's Fair, and the franchise which grew from that has never looked back. At that first Ripley exhibit – ironically under the overall theme of A Century of Progress – visitors could, besides much else, gasp at the Human Pincushion who never shed a drop of blood and seemed immune to torture; they could marvel as the Little Half Girl, born without arms or legs, used her mouth and stumps to write, thread needles and do jigsaw puzzles.[18] By 2014, seekers after the unusual and bizarre in ten different countries could add their number to the 12 million who have visited Ripley's 'Believe it or Not' emporia.

The largest of all is in London, a huge and indiscriminate collection that bears witness to both Ripley's own inexhaustible enthusiasm and the continuing appetite for his wares. Here's a giant portrait of Michelle Obama made entirely of bottle tops, there's an invitation to 'Fire Up Ol' Sparky!' and send 2,000 volts through the prisoner in the electric chair ('This interactive may not be suitable for young children'). Here an invitation to the funeral of the Duke of Wellington or a shrunken head, there a stuffed eight-legged Siamese piglet or a waxwork of 'the world's ugliest woman' (press the button at your own risk to see her face). The first exhibits a visitor sees are a taxidermied double-headed calf and cow with a horn growing out of its back. The last ones, presiding over the cafe, are waxworks of the world's tallest and fattest men, against whom we can measure and weigh ourselves. Along the way, Fyodor Jeftichew, brought from Europe to America by Barnum to become 'Jo-Jo, the dog-faced boy', stares out from the old photo to underline the family history of Ripley's show.

But these days, Ripley's human 'oddities' (at least the ones who come from close to home rather than distant, exotic tribes) bring a positive message. The film of the 'King of the Freaks' Johnny Eck, his torso ended just below his waist, celebrates 'a 60 year show-biz career'; as the rallying voice-over urges, 'Standing tall is nothing to do with your stature!' The video of Rose Siggins, who had the lower half of her body removed as a child as the result of sacral agenesis, emphasises the birth of her 'normal' child. The old freak show has become a vehicle for self-expression. The (waxwork) Vampire Woman, tattooed and implant-fanged, proclaims that she uses her body to encourage other women who have also been abused to stand up for themselves. On one continuously playing video, the 'Lizard Man' proudly displays his head to toe tattooed scales, his bifurcated tongue, his teeth filed to points and the word 'Freak' tattooed across his chest. And what's 'normal' anyway? 'You may not be the thinnest, tallest, fattest, smallest person in the world', rings Ripley's final message, 'but you might still have a special talent.' (Not everybody, you know, can roll their tongue into a tube.)

So the triggers for laughter change, in societies and individuals, too. And as they do, they continue to tell us something about our individual and collective selves. But underlying the changes, the question persists: what are we allowed to find funny? Ever since antiquity, the story of humour has also been the story of attempts to set limits to the permissible, and of humour's persistence in sneaking, sliding and blasting through every boundary set in its way. This push and pull, and its particular relevance for psychotherapists, are what the next chapter is about.

Notes

1 Beard 23.
2 Freud, 'Jokes' VIII:102.
3 Critchley 2.

4 Gutwirth 6.
5 Hobbes, *Elements* IX:13, *Leviathan* VI.
6 Beard 38.
7 Critchley 57; Hobbes *Leviathan* XIII.
8 Bremmer 13–14; Aristotle, *Poetics* III; Cook 4.
9 Bollas *Shadow*; Kalsched *Trauma* 18; Crowther and Schmidt 65.
10 Freud, 'Jokes' VIII.236.
11 Critchley 1; Cook 187; Critchley 87.
12 Tertullian in Carey 34–35.
13 Jacobson 167; Fiedler 47.
14 Critchley 72; www.academie-francaise.fr/le-dictionnaire.
15 Chesterfield XXXII.
16 Dickie 18–20, 46, 118.
17 Kathleen Jones 17; Fiedler 15.
18 www.cityclicker.net/chichfair/ripley.

Chapter 7

Shadow stories

Even 'superiority' theorists have their limits. Aristotle thought that while tragedy makes people out to be better than they are, comedy portrays them as worse; we laugh at what is ugly. But only, he adds, when this involves no pain or harm: the mask of comedy, he points out, is ugly and distorted, but it shows no pain. Hobbes, as we've seen, thought that laughing at the misfortunes of others told us as much about the laugher's own sense of inferiority as about humour itself. For him, one of the 'proper works' of greater minds is to 'help and free others from scorn'.[1]

The history of humour is also the history of attempts to control it. Ancient philosophers could find it incompatible with the seriousness of their purpose: the disciples of Pythagoras, for example, rather like the followers of Melanie Klein so many centuries later, were known for their lack of it. Plato would forbid laughter altogether to the Guardians of his ideal philosophical city, and humour has presented problems for seekers of the ideal ever since. 'Did Jesus laugh?' was a serious theological question for centuries. At the end of the fifteenth century, a document turned up which purported to be an eye-witness account of Jesus himself, and seemed to settle the debate. He was very beautiful, reported one Lentulus to Tiberius Caesar, with his wavy hair the colour of a ripe hazelnut, his bright eyes and mature and simple demeanour; he often smiled, and wept too. But no one had ever seen him laugh. Though each of the several versions of this document seems as apocryphal as the last, it perhaps tells something about an early Christian ideal of humour and its limits.[2]

Christianity itself rests on a radical act of folly, a complete overturn of the values of the mundane world. 'We are fools for Christ's sake', writes Paul to the Corinthians; it might look like folly indeed to endure persecution, to try to conciliate when slandered, to live homeless, ill-clad and buffeted, all in hope of a glorious hereafter. But 'God chose what is foolish in the world to shame the wise, God chose what was weak in the world to shame the strong' (1 Cor. 4:10; 1:28). Did Paul laugh as he said it, at the sheer absurdity of the idea? This foolishness, however, is about theology, not humour, in the same way that the tradition of the Holy Fool has little to do with wandering jokers and buffoons; both are beyond the scope of this book.

Nevertheless, the very absurdity of Paul's radical promise might be thought enough to evoke the laughter of sheer joy among believers, a lightness of heart that is of humour's essence. This is a long way from Tertullian's triumphant crow that we heard in the last chapter, and distinguishing the 'right' sort of humour from the 'wrong' became a question for theologians. Tertullian's near contemporary Clement shrank from the uncontrolled guffaw; he thought it sabotaged the measured flow of conscious human words that echoed the still abiding word of Christ within the soul. But he was not at all against a kindly joke to set young people at ease; he thought a gentle chuckle could echo the melodious sounds of the saints, 'harmoniously relaxing the austerity and over-tension of our serious pursuits'. Nearly two centuries on, however, St John Chrystostom might have been indignant to hear this: 'Christ is crucified, and dost thou laugh?' There would be time enough for laughter, he thought, when the soul reached heaven and saw the world for the vanity it was.[3]

From time immemorial, from Old Testament to New, this had been the predominant theme: laughter in a blessed future, suffering here on earth. As the book of Ecclesiastes reminds us, there is a time to laugh and a time to weep. 'I said of laughter "It is mad" and of pleasure, "What use is it?"', said the preacher. And 'sorrow is better than laughter, for by sadness of countenance the heart is made glad' (Ecc. 3:4; 2:2; 7:3). Early Christian teachers thought laughter betokened pride and evoked the admirable tears of the penitential saint. Idleness and laughter were the main enemies of the early monks, and monastic rules made laughter a punishable offence. In time, St Benedict's minutely detailed and widely followed Rule for monastic life sought a middle way: there should be no excessive or boisterous laughter, coarse jests or joking, but it was good to be cheerful. Yet the great abbess Hildegard of Bingen saw laughter as no more than a proof of our fallen state: in Eden, such had been the state of inner joy, that there was no need for it at all.[4]

Echoes of these ancient debates still linger in today's attempts to distinguish 'good' humour from 'bad', the kind that heals and brings people together from the kind that destroys and drives them apart. These are questions for therapists too, in their concerns for individuals' divided inner worlds and troubled relationships with outer ones. 'Avoid racist and sexist humour', advises Patch Adams, physician, social activist and clown; 'strive for goofiness and fun, not an endless string of jokes'. For over 40 years he has been donning his red nose and silly clothes to practise and teach not just medicine, but the physical and emotional benefits of the humour and 'silliness' that builds caring relationships and fosters happiness, kindness and good cheer. 'People crave laughter as if it were an essential amino acid', he writes. 'When the woes of existence beset us, we urgently seek comic relief.'[5] This was what he provided for more than a decade in the free hospital in his native West Virginia, and this is the message he and his associates at the Gesundheit! Institute still take to orphanages and other institutions, refugee camps and even war zones across the world. Many other people will know of Patch Adams through the 1999 movie, in which he was played by the acclaimed comedian and actor Robin Williams. The shock of Williams' suicide in 2014 dominated international headlines. Sometimes, perhaps, goofiness, red noses and fun may not be enough to counter the demons of depression, anxiety and fear of irreversible physical disease.

Sometimes something stronger may be needed. 'Why must it always be nice laughter, silliness, clowning about, goofing, that restores us to ourselves?' grumbled the British comic novelist Howard Jacobson after attending a conference on humour and healing. 'There can be no drawing of the lines with comedy. We cannot argue for its restorative powers and then pretend it is milk and water that restores us.' It wasn't just Marx Brothers films, he reminded his readers, that enabled Norman Cousins to laugh his way to health. He watched *Candid Camera* too – a long running television show that found much of its fun on both sides of the Atlantic by playing pranks on unsuspecting people and inviting the audience to laugh at their discomfiture. Cousins felt better because someone else felt worse.[6]

These days, many people in Britain at least are working to constrain humour's essential unruliness. The right-thinking consensus is wary indeed of anything that smacks of superiority or fun at the expense of someone it considers less privileged or fortunate than itself. Children are taught that they shouldn't laugh at those who are obviously 'different', or weaker, or otherwise disadvantaged. Schools engineer meetings between their pupils and these 'others' in an effort to counter stereotypes and prejudice that may have seeped through centuries. Children's entertainment has changed too. People purse their lips at the abusive marital relationship in which the traditional Punch and Judy have for centuries battled it out with a good mutual walloping. Contemporary sensibilities recoil from reminders of the freak-show. The 124 short actors assembled for the 1939 Wizard of Oz were given only a collective credit: 'Munchkins'. But Wikipedia now includes a roll-call of their names and, where known, their dates of birth and death. In Roald Dahl's classic morality tale *Charlie and the Chocolate Factory*, the factory's workforce of oompa-loompas were tiny folk, rescued from a wretched existence far away to relish the substance they craved in a mischievous and jolly servitude. By the time of the 1971 film version, there were few British actors short enough to play them; the cast of ten included a Maltese, a Turk and a German. In the 2005 re-make, thanks to computer technology, all 165 were played by a single actor, Deep Roy. In the musical version playing at Drury Lane in London since 2013, there are no short actors at all, only technical wizardry to make them appear so.[7]

So did you hear the one about the Englishman, the Irishman and the Scotsman? Not for much longer perhaps. Many people are now squeamish about what's known as ethnic humour; they worry about 'racist' jokes. They are taking a lot on here, for the depository of jests about the superiority of my folk over yours has been piling up since antiquity in most parts of the world, and travelling with remarkable ease between them. So, for instance, American jokes about stupid Poles overlap with Canadian ones about Newfoundlanders, and those the

English tell about the Irish, the French about Belgians and the Indians about Punjabis – and the ones the ancient Romans told about the citizens of Abdera in northern Greece as well.[8] There are some enduring modern categories: jokes about the canniness of Scots, for instance, are fairly international. But that hardly leaves the Scots defenceless: they find other people, especially the English, pretty risible too. And so do the Irish, for this sort of humour isn't just one-directional. As Simon Critchley puts it: 'the French laugh at the Belgians, the Belgians laugh at the Dutch and the Dutch laugh right back. The Danes laugh at the Swedes, the Swedes laugh at the Finns, and the Finns laugh right back.'[9] The exception to this robust international jostle is the one that makes people uneasy: Jews, like Scots, have an international reputation for canniness. But Jews are famously more likely to joke about each other than about anyone else. If a Gentile jokes about the Englishman, the Irishman and the Jew, should we be alerted to something else going on?

In Britain, critics of ethnic and 'racist' jokes may be touchy. They don't like being labelled 'politically correct', because they think that means people are laughing at them for being concerned with important political issues like the operation of anti-racist legislation, and for seeking to correct what they consider offensive to others as well as themselves. They may be right: people may indeed be laughing at their moral earnestness. And perhaps it's a good thing that people do? As a Jew, said Howard Jacobson in 1997, he feels far more threatened by those who would wipe out racist jokes than those who unthinkingly make them. For him, such jokes lance a boil, and so reaffirm social solidarity. And besides, 'we behave more intelligently than we talk'.[10] Jacobson seems to be pinpointing something important here, which would-be censors may miss: the lack of necessary causal connection between what we laugh at and what we do. The very cruelty of humour may expose our own – and by bringing it to awareness enable us to be more kind. If someone takes a tumble on that banana skin on the pavement, do passers-by really stand by and guffaw? Experience surely tells that they're far more likely to rush to their aid, an instance of Jacobson's reaffirmation of solidarity.

Throwing a custard pie, as Christie Davies points out in his major study of ethnic humour around the world, is not the same as throwing a hand grenade. If people are seriously anti-Semitic, as he says, they have far more deadly weapons than jokes to hand – abuse and slander, for a start. In general, Davies finds, ethnic jokes are an unreliable indicator about the tellers' feelings towards the people on the receiving end. These may range from dislike and hostility to amity and affection, and where there is a great deal of inter-group hostility, there may be no jokes at all. For Davies, jokes are social thermometers, not social thermostats: they provide valuable information about societies, but are emphatically not a tool for manipulating them. 'To become angry about jokes and seek to censor them because they impinge on sensitive issues is about as sensible as smashing a thermometer because it reveals how hot it is.' And besides this, he says, the would-be censors miss another important function of the ethnic joke: they enable people to accommodate and get along together in a world of industrial complexity and continual movements of populations. (Jews, for instance, make jokes about both ultra-Orthodoxy and assimilation.) 'Jokes', says Davies, 'are the balance in an unbalanced world.'[11]

And humour just goes on pushing the boundaries. Did you hear the one about how many Jews can fit into a Volkswagen? Answer: 506 – six in the seats and 500 in the ashtrays. In the 1980s there was a spate of such, collected from Germany, England, Sweden and different parts of the United States. In Germany the same sort of jokes were directed at immigrant Turks. Enabling people to get along together? The authors of this study suggest that 'Auschwitz jokes' can be seen as a collective attempt to come to terms with the enormity of the Holocaust.[12] If this is so, the attempt is far from over. These days, collectors of such jokes need only press a button on the computer to find a stack of them.

When do we laugh and where do we wince – and when would we impose an outright ban? Our senses of humour tell us about ourselves – and what they reveal about the shadow of our polished self-image may be shocking. Both revelation and shock are the very stuff of depth psychotherapy, the basic material which therapists and their clients work over as they try to bring hidden desires and hopes to light. Humour is on their side here, the uninvited guest which can catch them unawares and unprepared. First the laugh, then the unravelling of why it came: like a dream but more sudden, more visceral. Humour can sneak past the superego, evade the barriers of repression, and erupt from *somewhere else* to tell us that 'the Other' isn't just outside but within. We know how much disruption and shame the realisation may bring. The shadow is the repository of everything we reject. And yet this other self is also who I irrevocably am.

Psychotherapists know well the dangers of repressing and turning away from such uncomfortable truths, of too great a neurotic split between the conscious attitude and the energies of the unconscious. They know how insistently shadow selves may seek to become known to consciousness, and how the less their intimations are heeded, the more likely they are to burst out and elide the morally crucial distinction between fantasy and action, between the dark desire and its enactment. No one can be responsible for their unconscious selves; moral choice depends on knowing what we're deciding about. Here's one of psychotherapy's healing paradoxes: by (ideally at least) suspending moral judgement to enable revelation, it helps increase the sum of moral action in the world.

This may be far from easy, and for Jung at least there could be no definite 'technique' for achieving it. Rather, he thought, working with our shadow selves was like a long and difficult diplomatic negotiation. But it was worth it.

> The suffering shows the degree to which we are intolerable to ourselves. Agree with thine enemy, outside and inside! That's the problem! ... I admit it is not easy to find the right formula, yet if you find it you have made a whole of yourself, and this, I think, is the meaning of human life.[13]

In these often painful psychological negotiations, humour can give us the courage we need to get started. In his 1928 paper, Freud sought to unravel what made for its liberating and somehow elevating effect on the 'humourist'. Here's his example: a criminal is being led to the gallows on a Monday, and what he says is 'Well, this is a good beginning to the week!' Here, thought Freud, is 'the triumph of narcissism, the intimidated ego's victorious assertion of its own invulnerability.' And here, he thought, the super-ego is its (perhaps unexpected) friend, bringing 'kindly words of comfort', whether the humour concerns the subject's own self or other people. 'Its meaning is: "Look here! This is all that this seemingly dangerous world amounts to. Child's play – the very thing to jest about."'[14]

Humour can help us begin to face our fears not just of the world, but of our hidden selves. For that work even to begin, however, we need clues about whom and what we're dealing with. Self-knowledge begins in projection: what we find risible in others – their stupidity, their pompous rigidity, their distance from any number of imagined ideals – is the very thing that we may, with a rueful smile or even a surge of relief, one day accept about ourselves. Humour is one way of getting to that place, as professional comics know. 'Some of the stuff I do', says the British comedian Jack Dee, 'is releasing thoughts and ideas that the audience wouldn't usually be able to get away with, and the audience need you for that reason.' Another joker on the 'new comedy' circuit, Stewart Lee, recalls a joke he used to do about 'spastics'. (The very word!) And while some in the audience winced, people who actually had a child with disabilities would tell him just how true it was to their own experience: 'It's really nice to be able to laugh at the discomfort we feel.'[15] Maybe these professionals could teach psychotherapists a thing or two.

First the recognition, then the possibility of reflection, of putting together a fuller picture of who we are. As we saw in the first chapter, humour theorists like to talk about *gelasts* and *agelasts*, laughers and non-laughers. We can make a word-play here (and perhaps poke a little fun at the solemnities of theorising) by hearing 'elasticity', and thinking about the dangers of over-rigidity and the necessary psychological capacity to expand the boundaries of our permissible selves; we can remember the release of laughter's jelly-like wobbles. Humour loosens our moral stays; it helps us relax our judgements of our own imperfections – and so those of others too. As the American psychotherapist Thomas Moore puts it: 'One of the functions of humour, especially black humour, is to unlock the shadow from its imprisonment in some pious belief.'[16] Without this unlocking, an overly fixed and rigid attitude may be exploded by an autonomous eruption of shadow energy. 'I can't think what came over me', we say shamefaced, 'I never do something like that!' But we just have, the tenacity of the complex rendering us as limited in our psychological repertoire as Henri Bergson's mechanical automata were in their physical movement. This, for him, was laughter's task: to restore the flexible flow of psychological energy he called *élan vital*.

Humour can thieve the power of even the darkest sufferings. It can match the cruelty of experience with cruelty of its own, the black fixity of depression with its own blackness. In the old medical taxonomy, 'black humour' was the mark of the melancholic, the bitterness of bile. Like the alchemical Mercurius, it was both poison and panacea. Moore traces the old association of melancholy with the energy of the planet Saturn: 'It leads to a life of dryness, sadness, depression and inactivity; yet it is also a source of exalted genius and inspiration.'[17] Saturn both crushes life's energies and gives a structure to contain and shape their fuller expression. Without shadow, people, like paintings, are two-dimensional; it's by the lack of shadow that we know that what looks like a person is in fact a ghost. And it's when we can acknowledge the shadow that we can begin to see the light. As Jung puts it, 'One does not become enlightened by imagining figures of light, but by making the darkness conscious.'[18]

Then there may be surprises. We may fear the shadow as containing all we most reject. But for Jung, it also described the whole realm of the unconscious, which meant it carried a huge positive potential as well as darkness. Those dreams about the pursuing monster, the violent intruder, are the stuff of nightmare. But if on waking we can dare to face these figures and ask them what they want, we may learn more about the selves we have been excluding. And the recognition may bring surprising new energy. When we dare to give the threatening and repulsive old tramp of our dreams the glass of water he craves, then he may become a beautiful and laughing young boy. The shadow which is psychotherapy's raw material may turn out to yield, like the filthy confusion of the alchemists' *prima materia*, intimations of the psychological gold of greater individuation and wholeness. And then there may be another sort of laughter again.

This sort of psychological transformation might seem impossibly distant; just learning to carry the shadow in consciousness might seem burden enough. But as the American archetypal psychologist James Hillman saw it, this was only a step towards something else: learning to love it.

> At one moment, something else must break through, that laughing insight at the paradox of one's own folly which is also everyman's. Then may come the joyful acceptance of the rejected and inferior, a going with it and even a partial living of it. This love may even lead to an identification with and acting out of the shadow, falling into its fascination. Therefore the moral dimension can never be abandoned. Thus is cure a paradox requiring two incommensurables: the moral recognition that those parts of me are burdensome and intolerable and must change, and the loving, laughing acceptance which takes them just as they are, joyfully, forever. One both tries hard and lets go, both judges harshly and joins gladly.[19]

Is this capacity humour's greatest gift – to laugh lovingly with our own universally-human folly, even as we recognise the seriousness of our moral responsibility to self and others? Can we even imagine what a world of such citizens would be like? But at least humour can set us on the path. It can give initial courage to face the fear of hidden selves. It can nudge us towards discovering these, through recognising projections onto the objects of our mirth and derision. It can help to relax over-rigid attitudes and the grip of unconscious complexes. It can bring enough psychological distance from those complexes to allow for self-reflection, and ease us towards the blessed relief of self-acceptance. It can be a companion in exploring dark places which may turn out to contain potential for new and unexpected life. It can restore us to our fuller self and so to a sense of belonging, at last, with the rest of the human race, neither inflatedly better nor horribly worse than anyone else. And one more thing as well: humour brings the understandings of the 'talking cure' right down to earth, into our very nature as material human beings. This is what the next chapter is about.

Notes

1 Aristotle, *Poetics* V; Hobbes, *Leviathan* VI.
2 Sanders 136.
3 Clement in Brown 126, 134; Chrystostom in Sanders 125.
4 Hildegard in Sanders 129.
5 Adams 69, 65.
6 Jacobson 37.
7 www.theguardian.com/film/2005/jul/27/1.
8 Davies, *Ethnic Humour passim*; Beard 51.
9 Critchley 69.
10 Jacobson 33, 35.
11 Davies, *Ethnic Humour* 323, 8, 9, 308.
12 Dundas and Thomas 57–65.
13 Jung, *Letters 1* 234.
14 Freud, 'Humour' XX:220–221.
15 Dee in Cook 195; Lee in Cook 212.
16 Moore 92.
17 Ibid. 93–94.
18 Jung, 'The Philosophical Tree' 13:335.
19 Hillman 76.

Chapter 8

Bodies and brains

One thing we do know about Iambe, the serving woman who saved humans and the Earth itself from environmental catastrophe by making the goddess Demeter laugh. Iambe takes us to the heart of things. Sometimes she is called 'the limping one', because her name echoes the rhythm of the iambic poetic metre: one short syllable, one long, one short, one long. In ancient times, this was the rhythm of comic verse and, to this day, it's the most natural rhythm of speech in many languages, including English. Iambe measures the span of human life itself: the iambic thud-thud is the sound of the human heart, the first and the last sound we ever hear. No wonder that the iambic pentameter remains the basic unit of English verse, and others too: it contains as many heart beats as we make during a single breath.[1]

So Iambe tells us something about the place of humour in our heart-to-heart communications. This may be literal as well as metaphorical. When people experience negative emotions, it seems, their heart rhythms become erratic and disordered; when their emotions are positive, the rhythms become ordered and coherent. Other bodily systems also become synchronised; mind and body come into resonance: people feel 'together', 'good in their skin'. This seems to operate between people as well as within them. The heart beats of a loving couple may be as measurably synchronised during sleep as those between couples headed for divorce are discordant. (And don't people who have been happily married for many years often say that it's their sense of humour that's brought them through?)[2]

We can only imagine the heart-to-heart communication between Demeter and Iambe – or between psychotherapists and their clients during those unbidden 'states of grace'. But we know that in the ancient myth something transformative happened, just as it may in modern consulting rooms. What the many English translations of the myth emphasise is the quality of attention that Iambe brought to it: she's consistently described as sage, careful, trusty, thoughtful, diligent or perceptive. And then – something else bursts in, and humour shows another face entirely. Through the labyrinthine ways of mythic telling and retelling, thoughtful Iambe becomes conflated with another character whose name is Baubo. And though we can't be sure who she was – she appears here as a servant, there as a poor cottager, sometimes even as a queen – her transformative joke is always the same. Baubo lifts her skirts and flashes her genitals.

Baubo and her joke have a long and complex afterlife, and she has become a perfect hook for all manner of projections, often divided along gender lines. From the early Christian era on, she has been persistently associated with the greatest religious cult of the ancient world, the Mysteries of Eleusis (and we will hear more about this in Chapter 13). But Christian commentators had an interest in demonising the pagan mysteries – and woman's bodies as well. The story of Baubo became entangled with the long and anguished Christian attempt to foster 'masculine' spirit at the expense of 'feminine' matter and the attendant degradations of women and their role. From thoughtful and perceptive, Iambe/Baubo became a demon of the night, as squat and ugly as the toads and frogs who are her familiars.[3]

And then in 1898, a team of German archaeologists at Priene near Ephesus in Turkey turned up a group of statuettes in the remnants of an ancient temple of Demeter and her daughter Kore. These were of a form never seen before or since: little female figures whose heads and faces sat right at the top of their thighs, their vulva merging with their chins. They hold flowers, or baskets of fruit, or a lyre. The archaeologists called them Baubos and they have been perceived as almost anything from quaint and enchanting to monstrous and obscene. Views of Baubo herself have been as disparate. She seemed to make Jung uneasy: he evoked her as the opposite pole of the feminine archetype to the heavenly goddess, describing her once as symbol of the mother's unconscious will to power. For others, she remained a 'nasty old crone who had a weakness for exhibitionism'; as late as 1990 one male scholar was evoking the 'sordid story' of this 'insolent creature'. It took Winifred Lubell, in her passionate and detailed study published four years later, to reclaim Baubo, and place her honourably within the wide-reaching ancient veneration of female sexual energy and life-giving power. Lubell scorns the Priene images as 'the sacred made infantile and trivialised … obscene and enchanting dwarfs [which] seem to move uneasily between the profane and the pornographic'. For her, Baubo's gesture is entirely consistent with the iconic genital display of female divinity, from the prehistoric 'Venus of Laussel' to Hellenistic Isis and well beyond. The image endures into Christian times, reappearing in church carvings of Sheilagh-na-Gig made between the twelfth and sixteenth centuries, particularly in Ireland but in England and Wales as well. In 1842, George Lewis set about recording the profusion of carvings on the twelfth century church in Kilpeck in Herefordshire. In one grotesque and squatting figure, he saw a holy fool, 'the cut in his chest, the way to his heart, denotes it is always open to all and sundry'. What we see now is a Sheilagh, a female figure unmistakeably and gleefully pulling open her genitals as far as they will go. Baubo is reclaimed for contemporary women who rejoice in her earthiness, her belly laugh, her raucous delight in her own and humour's life-giving power.[4]

Here too is a reminder of the essentially embodied nature of humour, recognised in the medieval diagnoses of the fluxes and flows of our blood and phlegm, black and yellow bile. We laugh with the muscles of our ribcage, even until we (metaphorically) split our sides. Or until we (literally) start to leak through our bodily boundaries: we cry with laughter, we laugh until we wet ourselves. And what we've long laughed at is not just the refinements and cruelties of wit, but the body itself. The history of humour is rampant with ruderies, one long raspberry blown at those sensibilities which would rather the body didn't exist. As the philosopher George Steiner nicely puts it, 'There are no lavatories in tragic palaces, but from its very dawn, comedy has had use for chamber pots.'[5]

This is the realm of the Trickster, blundering, lying and cheating his amoral way through North American native creation myths and African and South Asian and Oceanic ones as well. Part human, part divine, now a coyote, now a raven or a hare, he can transform himself at will into any animal or a human being of any age and either sex. A voraciously hungry, rampantly phallic incoherence of detachable parts, he is the very image of the body's autonomy. When he covers the land with uncontrollable mountains of shit, body is all he is. But when he controls nature itself to acquire fire, water and even the sun for humankind, he is all creative spirit.[6]

Trickster is both a hero and the mocker mocked; he can die and come alive again. He reappears among the ritual clowns in different North American native tribes who brandish artificial penises and chuck buckets of excreta and mud in an eruption of scatology and sexual simulation. His detachable penis flies through time and space to become the medieval European jester's bladder and bauble, and later Mr Punch's big stick. Today's mockers mocked are circus clowns and slapstick comedians, sending up the absurdities of social pretention while also making us laugh at them for getting the material world so wrong as they trip over themselves and the furniture, still sloshing buckets of stuff about.

Just why have so many different peoples at so many different times found so much humour in such antics? It seems a bit risky to impute motive to people whose cultures are so distant from our own; it seems a bit easy to see all such humour as no more than a release of psychological energy, or a sanction to take time off from good behaviour, or a brief release from social taboos so as better to observe them. Perhaps we might also imagine that by bringing us so relentlessly back to bodily basics, this type of humour brings us to something more psychologically complex and perplexing: the essentially paradoxical nature of the human creature. The conscious mind may tell us we're in control; the body can show us at any minute that we are not. There seems no limit to the soarings of the human imagination; our animal nature reminds us that limited is exactly what we are. By acting out the drama, humour can help us negotiate the endlessly re-opening gaps between aspiration and actuality, romance and reality, and help us live more good-humouredly with ourselves. Here, from ancient Sumeria and around 4,000 years ago, comes what may be the world's oldest recorded joke: 'What has never occurred since time immemorial? A young woman who did not fart in her husband's lap.'[7]

What does it mean to be human? When once asked about 'the therapy of individuation', Jung rather testily replied: 'It is not a therapy. Is it therapy when a cat becomes a cat? It is a natural process.'[8] But a natural process towards what? The negotiation of our animal and distinctly human selves has been one of humour's abiding preoccupations, from Trickster's human–animal transformations to the ass's ears and cockscombs of medieval jesters and well beyond. Aristotle thought that laughter was one of the distinguishing characteristics of human beings: a child, he said, became human when it first laughed, 40 days or so after its birth. Ancient Romans laughed a great deal at monkeys when they imitated humans, both because they were so like us, and, importantly, because they were only acting as if they were: *they seemed human but they weren't.*[9] Even 50 years ago British children were still being presented with the same conundrums about the distinctions between humans and other animals. Zoos would put on chimpanzees' tea parties for our delight, dressing them up in human clothes and sitting them at tables with all the tea-time paraphernalia. I remember the excitement, the anxiety that we might miss even a minute of it. I can remember how funny it was – and how disconcertingly *odd*, because of course sitting down at their tea party wouldn't be the least bit like sitting down at Granny's. These days, laughter is thought to bring us closer to our primate ancestors rather than help us distinguish ourselves from them. It's thought to derive from their 'open mouth' signalling of submission, non-hostility and a desire to play. But a century and more of depth psychological theories have also taken us away from our animal kinship: these days, a human's 'natural' development is generally understood to be a great deal more vulnerable to damage and interruption than a cat's.

So the questions are age-old: what are the limits of humanness, what distinguishes humans from other animals? The question was encoded in the motley band of dwarfs and others who looked so obviously 'different' as they tumbled their way through the centuries; it was repeated through the circus freak-shows as they elided the differences between humans and other animals to display the 'Dog-faced Boy' or the 'Mule Faced Woman'. These days in Britain, we don't have to visit Ripley's to bring questions of human limits right back home and into our bodies and minds. In the space of two weeks at the beginning of 2015, a mainstream British television channel showed these programmes: an episode in a series that followed the dating attempts of people whose obvious physical, intellectual or emotional 'differences' had made it hard for them to find a partner; part of a series that graphically explored extreme and often regretted 'cosmetic' body alterations; and a one-off story about 'Britain's fattest people'. The programmes, as the commercial sponsor's advertisement introduced them, were about 'changing perceptions'; they seemed designed to elicit sympathy, in an invitation to look beyond the differences to find a shared humanity.[10] If viewers laughed instead at frailties which were not their own – and participants in these programmes certainly knew what it was to be laughed at – had the programmes failed? Or were the viewers eased through laughter towards a wider understanding of the varieties of human expression?

What does it mean to be human? 'Only connect', said the English novelist E.M. Forster at the beginning of the twentieth century. It could be a handy slogan – for a greetings card, an invitation to become a friend on social media or a community outreach programme. But Forster meant something rather different. 'Only connect' was Margaret Schlegel's project in *Howard's End* for the man who had just agreed to marry, Henry Wilcox, drawn up after he had surprised her with a kiss that seemed completely cut off from his everyday self. 'Only connect', she thought,

> the prose and the passion, and both will be exalted and human love will be seen at its height. Live in fragments no longer. Only connect, and the beast and the monk, robbed of the isolation that is life to either, will die.[11]

The project was not very successful. Mr Wilcox appeared cheerful, reliable and brave, says Forster; but inside it was chaos, ruled if at all by a belief, reinforced by conventional religious education, that bodily passion was bad. Wilcox was not, however, as he said of himself, a fellow who bothered about his own inside. And Margaret was too intellectual and idealistic altogether. Perhaps her project would have been more successful if she'd had more of a sense of humour.

A hundred years on, when our own 'inside' seems to have lost so many of its physiological and psychological mysteries, the Wilcoxes' dilemmas may seem quaint indeed. But wouldn't many psychotherapists still readily recognise their difficulties in relating to themselves and each other? Human beings are still Forster's beasts and monks, creatures of animal bodies and instincts and soaring minds. Helping people to hold these opposites of their nature has been the stuff of depth psychotherapy ever since Freud first set out to 'raise hell' by bringing the dark depths of human passions and desire into conscious light. But the psychotherapeutic project has also encoded a certain imbalance. Freud's early work with women whose distress was expressed through their suffering 'hysterical' bodies seemed to work because it enlisted their intellectual understanding to restore them to health. Mind over matter: much psychotherapeutic theory and practice carries that message. So practitioners of the 'talking cure' and its derivatives have traditionally not been very good at *bodies*. As the American Jungian analyst Donald Kalsched, widely known for his work on early trauma, puts it: the whole field has historically been preoccupied with 'disembodied insight and excessively left-brain dominated "interpretations"', with Jungian analysis 'especially guilty of this ascent into mentalisation and the pursuit of intellectual meaning'.[12]

In this, depth psychology has been part of a far larger and longer project altogether. The honouring of mind and spirit over body and matter could be a shorthand description of the development of 'Western civilisation', with all its attendant glories and ills. Christianity's long-lasting dis-ease with humour and laughter was in part at least a revulsion from their essential, and uncontrollable, embodiment in matter. Once, the world seemed otherwise. The ancient Greek tragedies needed no lavatories, and their portrayal of moral and spiritual suffering offered little humour either. But the satyr plays which always followed them were a rampant riot of boozy lusting after sex, grub and the hunt. In the one play that survives complete, the *Cyclops* of Euripides, the main jokes revolve round eating, farting, cooking and belching. These are stories, as the British classicist Edith Hall says, about men behaving badly; for her, they restore a masculine collective consciousness after the tragedies' unsettlings.[13] But satyrs aren't quite men either. Followers of Dionysus, god of dissolution, they blur the categories of human and beast with their tails and hoofs and pointy ears. They are cunning and innocent, stupid and knowing, child-like and bald. We can imagine Trickster roistering in among them, a gleefully insistent reminder that the human spirit is housed in mammalian body, and that both tragedy and comedy are equally part of the human lot.

But that tragi-comic balance didn't last. The Romans trimmed the satyrs' horns, shortened their tails and penises and turned them into fauns. By the end of the fifteenth century, Botticelli was depicting the Taming of the Centaur – half-man, half-horse – by the goddess Athena. Their apparently playful flirtation as she reaches out to tousle his hair shouldn't deceive anyone: this was an allegory of the Triumph of Chastity over Lust, of Wisdom's Taming of Brute Force. Soon afterwards, Albrecht Durer's engraving shows satyr as family man, watching proudly over wife and baby. If it weren't for their woodland habitat and animal pelt of a blanket, and her rather strange ears, his wife and baby would be very nearly human. You can tell it: these satyrs are good enough parents.

This civilising socialisation is inescapably part of psychotherapy's task – a microcosmic, individual version of that macrocosmic, collective process. A generation ago and perhaps even lingeringly now, the talking cure was often derided as a self-indulgence, a licence to discover what you really, really wanted – and then to go for it and blame your parents. In fact, the very opposite is so: psychotherapy is based on a fundamental expectation that the dangerous chaos of the instinctual world, once named, can be tamed to come under conscious adult control. The most common central theme of psychodynamic therapy today is explicitly *developmental*. It imagines individual childhoods as the cause of adult sufferings; it helps people construct healing fictions of how they arrived where they are, in the hope that they will become more of what they could be. Somewhere in there is an implication that this re-membered child will *grow up better*. When psychotherapists speak of 'reclaiming the inner child', they are most usually talking about the playfulness, spontaneity and eagerness for discovery which upbringing may have prematurely quashed, not the little Trickster's amoral, undifferentiated mass of appetites. We need the image of the child, says Jung, to 'compensate or correct, in a meaningful manner, the inevitable one-sidedness and extravagances of the conscious mind'. But it is not the actual child he is talking about, rather the symbolic one who carries our psychological future and personifies as yet unconscious possibilities of individuation. For Jung, the Trickster personifies an earlier stage of human consciousness, a forerunner of alchemical Mercurius in all his craftiness; he still lives in the collective shadow and demands our attention lest he be acted out in unconscious projection. But this Trickster shows signs of growing up too; by the end of the Winnebago cycle of his stories, Jung finds him 'quite useful and sensible'.[14]

How could we wish it otherwise? We don't have to believe in Jung's collective unconscious to see evidence in the manifold brutalities of the world that the human race has far to go before it grows up into responsible adulthood. 'Civilisation' can seem a thin veneer, both collectively and individually. Maybe that's one reason that so many children, and adults too, don't laugh at clowns at all, but instead are repelled and frightened enough to earn themselves an official classification as *coulrophobics*. The clown's clumsiness and rudery may be too uneasy a reminder of what we are supposed to have grown out of; his outsized shoes and baggy clothes suggest we may not even now have reliably grown into the competencies and self-restraint that social being demands. (And why does the clown seem so sad under his painted smile?) Monkeys are easier altogether. Children of all ages can relish their matter-of-fact abandon to bodily enjoyments because although they may be doing things that we might like to, we know that in the end they are *not like us* and operate by different rules. Besides, they're usually safely behind bars.

'Civilisation' and its values may sometimes seem precarious. But ironically, those very values may have contributed to rendering it so apparently fragile. The cost of centuries of over-reliance on the capacities of mind and rationality, of often active warfare against the instincts and the body, has become apparent. Mind and matter have become uncoupled and the physical world itself is suffering. The lament is familiar, yet still it acts itself out not just on the earth but in individual bodies, as 'the diseases of civilisation' multiply. There's talk in Europe and North America of an 'epidemic' of childhood obesity. Elsewhere the changing climate condemns others to starvation. Psyche suffers: the archetypal dream of individual and collective wholeness seems further away than ever as people are cut off from the sense of what Kalsched calls an 'indwelling', embodied soul.[15] There can seem little cause for humour in the world. Indeed, the very capacity for humour may appear to be under threat.

In his monumental survey *The Master and His Emissary*, psychiatrist and philosopher Iain McGilchrist brings us right back into the structure of the human brain to tell a cultural history of the glories and dangers of 'Western civilisation'. These days, as he says, neuroscientists have largely stopped hypothesising about the differences between the brain's left and right hemispheres, since it has become apparent that every identifiable human activity is served at some level by both. They have been discouraged too by the way scientific work has passed into popular descriptions of the left hemisphere as 'masculine', hardnosed, logical, realistic and dull and the right as 'feminine', dreamy, sensitive, creative and exciting. But for McGilchrist, the functions of and relationship between the two hemispheres remain of fundamental importance in understanding not just the human creature but the kind of world that humans create. The hemispheres have worked together, he says, to give us the most precious of human gifts: reason and imagination. But after 500 years of 'Western culture', he finds, they have become dangerously out of kilter. The left hemisphere 'emissary' has forgotten that it is there to serve its right hemisphere 'master', and the vital relationship between the two is lost.[16]

McGilchrist conjures a chilling vision of what the world would look like if the functions he associates with the left hemisphere managed more or less to suppress those of the right. At the limit, we would lose the capacity to see the patterns and relationships which make up a whole, but focus instead on the mass of detailed parts in isolation. We would find it harder and harder to live with ambiguity and possibility, novelty and uncertainty; we would lose the capacity for metaphor. We would understand the world increasingly through theories and abstractions rather than context – which would mean, among other things, that we would lose the capacity for humour, because humour depends vitally on being able to understand the context of what is being said and done. Our very sense of our own essential nature would change: we would see each other as representatives of categories rather than as individuals. And inevitably, the capacity for relationship would profoundly suffer. The feelings, needs and expectations of others would no longer matter to us; we would lose the capacity to empathise, or even to interpret non-verbal messages. Communication of feelings would become hugely problematic: we would become less adept at both conveying and recognising the facial expressions that carry emotion, including humour, smiling and laughter, as well as the peculiarly human ability to express sadness through tears. At the limit, we would lose the capacity to understand the boundary between self and other.[17]

This grim picture is hardly a prediction, and an equally chilling vision could be constructed of a world in which the capacities and skills associated with the right hemisphere were deprived of the ordering capacities of the left. The sets of skills are necessarily complementary. The right hemisphere needs the left, McGilchrist emphasises, if it is to 'unpack' and make sense of experience. The left depends on the right's direct contact with the embodied, lived world if its own abstraction is to return to living experience. Left hemisphere division must continually return to right hemisphere unity and a new, 'higher' level of synthesis. Without this virtuous spiral of union, division and re-union, crucially made possible by the faculty of creative imagination, it's hard to see how, in McGilchrist's thesis, humans could develop at all. Yet the earlier maturing right hemisphere is primary. For him, it is more involved in 'almost every aspect of the development of mental functioning in early childhood and of the self as a social, empathic being'. From the start, it's the right hemisphere's capacity to identify the expression of emotion in an individual face that underlies the child's growing sense of identity through interaction with the face of the mother. Through life, it's the right hemisphere which gives us a sense that we are an embodied self; without it, our memories would become more concerned with facts in the public domain than those which are personal or emotionally charged. The right hemisphere is concerned with the meaning of language rather than simply its form and system. It helps us to be realistic about ourselves and how we stand in relation to the world. Importantly, it enables us to suffer our own sadnesses and those of others, when the left hemisphere would deny them. Without the functions of the right hemisphere, in short, we would no longer 'be ourselves'. People with right hemisphere damage do in fact report a 'foreignness' of the self, a sense of disconnection from the world. Activation of the left hemisphere in people who are especially prone to dissociation results in faster than usual inhibition of the right.[18]

Neuroscientists might baulk at McGilchrist's conclusions. But many psychotherapists would recognise immediately in his description of right hemisphere functions the very capacities which often seem painfully damaged in their patients and clients. Donald Kalsched, to take just one instance, has linked McGilchrist's thesis with the dissociative defences he finds in patients who suffer from early relational trauma. These defences, says Kalsched, develop as a 'self-care system' to protect the very core of their self from further violation. But what they may also do is work against 'wholeness' by impeding the essential integration of the brain hemispheres, or even damaging the right one. This leaves the trauma encoded in the right hemisphere untouched, and a crucial therapeutic task is to encourage the right-brain to right-brain communication which will reach and so heal it.[19] As Chapter 11 further explores, this is not the only implication for their own theories and practice that psychotherapists have found in the neuroscientific work which has burgeoned in recent years. For its own part, neuroscience has edged towards the insights of psychotherapy to explore how mental meaning may affect brain processes and the talking cure lead to measurable brain changes. There is even a nascent academic discipline called 'psychodynamic neuroscience', devoted to exploring the age-old conundrum of the mind–brain relationship – and by extension the relationship of both with the body as well. As Aikaterini Fotopoulou puts it in her introduction to a recent collection of essays that grew out of two years of exploratory seminars between psychoanalysts and neuroscientists: 'It is now increasingly seen that emotions and motivation also define mental abilities, embedded in the acting, sensing and feeling body and subject to intricate couplings between organisms and their interpersonal, social and technological environments.'[20]

But, Fotopoulou emphasises, this 'new' science faces 'vast unknowns'. Her collection is called *From the Couch to the Lab*. Given the estimate that there are more connections within the human brain than there are particles in the known universe, a 100-billion nerve cells making a 100-trillion interconnections, it seems safe to assume that it will be a while yet before the messages from couch to lab (and back again) come clear. But people are working on it. Already by 2004, the gigantic American Society for Neuroscience annual meetings drew some 30,000 researchers.[21] Ten years later, there were a clear thousand more, each and every one of them exploring some aspect of the functions and dysfunctions of the brain. A perfect image of the left brain's discriminating attention to the amassing of detail in the pursuit of clarity and certainty?

Iain McGilchrist sees hope in the fact that the way the left brain perceives the world, as forever progressing in a single straight line, simply isn't the way the world actually is. As he points out, there are no straight lines in nature, only curves. The right brain's way suggests a circle: it sees 'in the round' and its cognition progresses not by adding sequential segments, but by bringing something into focus within a whole that can encompass opposites.[22] Trickster lived in a cyclical world too. Dismembered, re-membered, dead and resurrected, shape-shifting into a myriad of opposites and containing them all, Trickster, like the human brain and mind, is also is a creator of the world. So are humour and laughter, and the following chapters explore their possible place in the consulting room. But first, a pause on the threshold.

Notes

1 Warner 152; Byatt in Wood and Byatt xv.
2 Institute of HeartMath, quoted in Donleavy and Shearer ch. 4.
3 Lubell for details on Baubo in this and next paragraph.
4 Jung, 'The Syzygy' 9ii:24; 'Psychological Aspects of the Mother Archetype' 9i:167; Olender 91; Lubell 103; Lewis quoted in Jacobson 58.
5 Steiner 247.
6 Details on Trickster in this and next paragraph from Apte, Radin.
7 McDonald, personal communication 31 August 2008.
8 McGuire and Hall 206–207.
9 Beard ch. 7.
10 Channel 4: *The Undateables*, *Shut Ins: Britain's Fattest People*, *Bodyshockers: Nips, Tucks and Tattoos*.
11 Forster 174–175.
12 Kalsched *Trauma* 8.
13 Edith Hall 142–169.
14 Jung, 'Child Archetype' 9i:276, 'Trickster' 9i:477, 484.
15 Kalsched *Trauma* 19.
16 McGilchrist 1–2, 13–14.
17 Ibid. 49–61, 82–90.
18 Ibid. 88, 66, 54, 70–71, 84, 236.
19 Kalsched *Trauma* 176, 231–232.
20 Fotopoulou *et al.* 27.
21 Rose 3–4.
22 McGilchrist 446 *et seq.*

In the consulting room

Chapter 9
Thresholds

As initiates and officials of Demeter's great Mysteries processed along the Sacred Way from Athens to Eleusis, they passed a small river that marked the boundary between the two cities, with a bridge above it. Just there, their mood was shattered by a gaggle of grotesquely masked buffoons, who jeered from the bridge at their ceremonial solemnity and cavorted about with lewd gestures and jokes. It's tempting to find Baubo among them, and she would certainly have been at home there, for before the iambic became the general rhythm of comedy, it was the metre specific to invective poetry and lampoon. There was nothing sweet about its barbs either: when its master practitioner Archilous died, people trod softly near his tomb lest they disturb the wasps that nested there.[1]

The mockers at the bridge were no gatecrashers. They were an intrinsic part of the rite and they seemed to mark the crossing of a boundary that was more than geographic. Once the great procession had passed the bridge, it seems, the atmosphere changed and the most secret and holy part of the ten-day celebration began. At that point, a threshold had been crossed between secular and sacred space. The mockers appeared at precisely this demarcation: they held both the boundary between secular and sacred and the bridge from first to second.[2]

At many other such thresholds, and across times and cultures, buffoonery and mockery have also seemed as essential as they were to the Eleusinian Mysteries. Ritual foolery has been intrinsic to rites of mediation between human and divine in many parts of the world. Pueblo Indians perform sacred dances that enact their gods – and clowns burlesque the whole procedure, stumbling among them and making obscene comments. Among the Zuni, clowns mock ceremonial communication with the deities by pretending to telephone them. Where religions meet, the old ways may become incorporated into the new. The Christianised Mayo of Mexico who re-enact during Lent the Stations of the Cross are accompanied by clowns who mockingly 'worship' their own idols and pretend to catch and eat excreta from the kneeling pilgrims.[3]

Christian Europe had its own versions of mayhem around its sacred thresholds, particularly at the turn of the year. At Christmas-tide, the medieval Church appointed a Boy Bishop who superintended the commemoration of Herod's slaughter of the first-born after Jesus's birth. The ritual was intended to enjoin humility; it emphasised the purity and innocence of childhood and enacted a reminder of Jesus's injunction to 'become as little children'. But humour is not so easily directed. As time went on, this decorous evocation of Christianity's inversion of worldly values exploded irresistibly into a Feast of Fools which inverted the rituals of the Church itself. In France especially, grotesque masqueraders danced and bawled indecent songs in the middle of services, ate blood sausages in parody of the Mass, burned stinking incense made of shoe leather and brayed like asses where they should have prayed. In one notorious monastery, the kitchen staff dressed themselves in priestly garb turned inside-out and capered about reading upside-down bibles thorough spectacles made of orange peel.[4]

People loved this sort of sport, they relished the mayhem and topsy-turvy chaos, and authority's efforts to suppress it were slow to succeed. Once outlawed by the Church, the mayhem just erupted in different, secular forms. In France, societies of fools paraded the streets, mocked the great and the good, and exposed their corruptions, sometimes dealing out a rough justice of their own. In England, the authorities tried and tried again to put an end to this sort of revelry. In the middle of the sixteenth century, there was a law to ban offensive jokes about the Eucharist; then a royal injunction tried to suppress jokes against the clergy; then yet another law forbade joking references to God on stage. But none of this really worked: students at different universities and the Inns of Court still rejoiced in bawdy parodies of the rituals of the Church. Later still, mayhem moved with the travelling parties of masked guisers and mummers who burst unannounced into rich houses at Christmas-tide. Menace was never far below the jokey surface: they sometimes broke down unwelcoming doors and demanded hospitality and cash before they would leave.[5]

The tension between chaotic exuberance and official attempts at control seemed irreconcilable and, to this day, something of the old chaos still erupts around the holy thresholds of the Christian year. They're there in the pantomimic excesses played out as part of the traditional English Christmas-tide and the carnival that in many countries precedes the austerities of Lent; there are traces in the Mayday mummeries that in England still usher in the once-holy month of Mary. The old negotiation between secular chaos and sacred order seems archetypal, built into our psychic natures, even if its origins and history are forgotten. English carol singers still innocently echo the undertow of menace, as they bring the good tidings of Christmas and insistently demand their figgy pudding in return:

>We won't go until we've got some
>We won't go until we've got some
>We won't go until we've got some
>So bring us some here.

The old seasonal excesses have been widely interpreted, rather as the bodily exuberances of the last chapter but on a larger, more contained and ritualised scale, as social safety valves. They made possible, it's said, the maintenance of a social order ordained first by the Church and then by civic authorities. Their unpredictable exuberance may seem a world away from psychotherapy's carefully ordered conventions of time and place. Mockery and menace have no place at all in therapeutic technique, and when they erupt can seem nothing but destructive; many psychotherapists will remember how the persistent mockery of their most careful interventions signalled an irreparable breakdown of trust between themselves and a patient.

But seen through another lens, the old topsy-turvy inversions of the established order may also have something to say about therapeutic work. To step from the everyday world into the consulting room is also to cross a threshold from the secular into a sacred space, where therapists try to leave behind their 'ordinary' life in the service of a relationship that allows 'something other' to be revealed, and where patients may hope to find acceptance of their hidden and shameful selves. When the initiates of the Mysteries crossed the border between Athens and Eleusis, they left behind the certainties of civic life and opened themselves to the radically unknown. In the consulting room too, the certainties of conscious attitudes meet the unknown of the unconscious to reveal aspects of ourselves – whether therapist or patient – that we may joyfully embrace or, like the old forces of law and order, try painfully to deny. Dreams may insist that nothing in our human nature can be alien to the work: bodies may leak, lavatories overflow and piles of shit build up in the beautiful ballroom to remind us of aspects we could rather forget. Learning to negotiate a personal world turned upside down may become the very stuff of psychotherapy's task. Dreams blur even the boundaries that seem most settled: when they give women a penis and men a vagina, they can intimate, just as surely as did the exuberant cross-dressing of the old topsy-turvydom, that we are all both masculine and feminine, male and female. Dreams can be funny, too: in their delightfully well-chosen incongruities and the apt wit of their puns it's hard not to see humour at work, and an invitation to find it in our waking lives. In the consulting room as in the old customs, humour can ease connections between the ordinary of everyday and the unknown that lies beyond.

But first, people have to get across the threshold. It may be hard sometimes for psychotherapists to remember just how frightening the first step into therapy may be for people who come to consult them, just how little they know what to expect from this new sort of encounter. But here is 'Margery', bereft and socially isolated after the death of her husband when she was 70 years old. She'd been diagnosed with depression and found herself referred to the British National Health Service for weekly psychotherapy with 'Dr Grey'. The first session was, by her account, a formality. It was with the second that the therapy 'proper' began.

> I just went in and he said 'Good morning' and then he said 'Sit down'.... And there was silence!... I hadn't the faintest idea what I was supposed to

say. I'd already explained to him my situation, how it had come about, but what more could I say? And this went on for practically the whole session.... I went out of the room very concerned, very disturbed. I couldn't just say 'What's going on, why you don't talk to me?' – well, I just couldn't. I mean, here's somebody who's a psychiatrist; you think he knows what's happening, he knows what we should be doing. But surely, when it's a new patient who's never been in therapy before and hasn't the faintest idea what it's all about – somebody at least ought to say 'Well, look, don't be surprised if I don't speak to you, I'm just waiting for you to say the first thing that comes into your head.' Because it just makes your brain seize up, and you can't think of anything, not a thing!

As the therapy began, so it went on, as Margery's longing for love latched ever more firmly on to the one person she hoped would offer it, and was met in return with the silences of Dr Grey. Four years later, for some time already paying privately for a weekly session, Margery still found the very thought of ending the relationship intolerable. It doesn't do to diagnose from her account just what this was all about. But we can perhaps wonder whether that initial threshold-crossing established a pattern of longing and its frustration that neither party seemed able to move beyond.[6]

It is nearly 30 years since Margery recounted her continuing ordeal. But how much has changed? A decade later, the English psychoanalyst Nina Coltart was wondering just what had happened to 'ordinary good manners' at the threshold of the consulting room. She was writing particularly about the careful shaping of an assessment interview, designed to guide potential patients on elsewhere for a continuing therapy. But, as she pointed out, any first meeting is also an 'assessment', and here too 'the subsequent treatment is likely to proceed with less difficulty if its jumping-off point feels good'. She herself had heard so many distressing accounts of first meetings from bruised patients that she could only conclude that manners were too often abandoned at the consulting room door. She herself always, for instance, took care to introduce herself by name with a handshake and to acknowledge by name the person she was meeting; she showed them where the lavatory was and accompanied them to the consulting room, indicating where they should sit. She spelled out such simple courtesies because she knew that many therapists simply didn't offer them – and that the lack of them made a painfully marked impression on people already vulnerable and anxious. She recalled, for instance, a young analyst, reporting on a preliminary interview, who laughed as she recounted how a new patient came in and, knowing no better, went straight to sit in the analyst's own chair. 'Of course I had to move her.' Coltart did not find this at all funny, and imagined that for the patient it must have been even less so.[7]

And while she was on the subject, she wanted to know something else: whatever happened to smiling? There appeared to be an extraordinarily powerful, if unspoken, myth that to smile at a patient was to do something 'mysteriously awful'. This seemed to her both ridiculous and sad, when an ordinary smile could so quickly enable the patient to relax.

> A welcoming smile at the beginning, and an occasional laugh if humour seems important to the patient – even more strongly taboo in some quarters – need not betoken an attitude inimical to the assessor's dignity, or that we know the patient is here because he is suffering in some way. Why can't a smile be a small but vital part of the ordinary good manners required by the act of inviting someone to sit down in one's own room to tell one private things about himself?[8]

Well, that was 20 years ago. But it wasn't long ago at all that the Jungian psychiatrist and analyst Jean Knox was reporting a colleague's memory of her own first meeting with a therapist. To me, this account conjured immediately a set of stage directions – as perhaps in a sense it was, a scenario carefully prepared by one of the protagonists. *Scene: Evening, an unfamiliar part of London. The therapist opens the door, but beyond establishing the visitor's name, says nothing. She ushers her into a shabby and depressing room, and indicates the chair (low and hard with a padded seat) on which she should sit; she herself sits down some distance away. Her face is expressionless. Silence.*

The would-be patient remembers how the scene unfolded:

> I felt more and more uncomfortable, feeling vulnerable and small. Eventually I realised that she expected me to talk, so I began to fill what felt like the vast chasm between us. But I soon began to feel that I was babbling. I wasn't getting any feedback ... I was disoriented.... When the session ended, I felt bad. I thought I must be a very inadequate sort of analysand. I had not done it well. There was something wrong with me. I was pathetic and stupid.

The prospective patient eventually got angry at what she saw as a lack of kindness and understanding. This first scene was also the last, for she never went back. Experiences of this sort, Knox found, were not uncommon: many of her colleagues had seen patients who reported similarly distressing encounters.[9]

For some psychotherapists, this sort of therapeutic persona or mask may be both theoretically justified and an important part of technique: for them, it expresses the neutrality and objectivity of the therapist which are so necessary to induce the transference, particularly of the negative sort, that is key to their work. But the problem with any rigidly applied technique – as the bruising experience of these patients eloquently shows – is that one size simply doesn't fit all. What may be meat and drink to one relationship may be crushing in another, simply exacerbating the painful feelings of inadequacy and vulnerability which brought the patient into therapy in the first place. And not all of them, their confidence undermined by the very first meeting, may feel able to leave right then.

The brilliant French mime Marcel Marceau once made his own inimitable comment on the dangers of too-rigid a persona. He evoked a clown-like figure coming back to his dressing room at the end of his act, negotiating the threshold back to ordinary life. As he shrugged off bits of imagined costume, you could see him beginning to relax, glad that one more show was over. And then, he made to take off his smiling mask. But it wouldn't come away from his face. He squeezed and pushed at it, then tore. His whole person conveyed his mounting panic, a desperate contrast to his still-smiling face. I can't even remember how the act ended. Perhaps it was too painful.

In some therapeutic quarters, the very notion of persona, at least the one worn by patients rather than therapists themselves, seems to have acquired rather a bad name; persona seems to have become equated with a sort of 'false self' that needs to be replaced by a more flexible expression of the amplitude of patients' 'real' natures. But in the complex interactions between private and public worlds, we all need a persona, or rather a wardrobe of personae, through which to communicate what we choose of ourselves in different situations and at different times. Without persona, social relationships would founder and our 'real selves' would be too exposed altogether: we would hardly want the bank manager to whom we're applying for a loan to see the vulnerability and self-doubt we may entrust to an intimate. So the persona is designed both to make a particular impression on other people and to conceal aspects of ourselves from their view. 'That the latter function is superfluous', says Jung,

> could be maintained only by one who is so identified with his persona that he no longer knows himself; and that the former is unnecessary could only occur to one who is quite unconscious of the true nature of his fellows.[10]

So psychotherapists as much as their patients need persona. The question for both is how much of their 'real selves' they will reveal. Psychotherapy's relationships are built on acceptance of asymmetrical self-revelation. But how rigid and unvarying need the therapist's persona be? For Nina Coltart at least, therapists' unsmiling masks seemed more likely to be about a rather precarious sense of themselves than the proper demands of their task.

Many of the people who seek therapy may also bring a precarious sense of themselves, a sense that the face they present to the world is beginning to slip. Jung would have thought this a better therapeutic starting point than a belief that their mask is a perfect expression of who they are. 'If people are identical with [the mask], they can do nothing but live their biography', he said; it is in this discrepancy between the public face and the private reality that neurosis can begin. For him, it is when people can step easily in and out of social role as the situation demands that there is room for psychological growth towards greater wholeness.[11] Perhaps it is when both parties in the therapeutic relationship are more able to play with their different masks that growth of and in the therapeutic relationship can really flourish.

Then people may find that persona may reveal rather than neurotically restrict. It was through mask that the ancient Greek actors were able to intimate archetypal levels of emotion and bring audiences to their own deep realisations about what it means to be human. Some masks express tragedy. But others emphatically do not, for we are creatures of life's comedies too, and mask has always been intrinsic to comedy's play, at thresholds and elsewhere. In his influential study of late medieval carnival, *Rabelais and His World,* the Russian philosopher Mikhail Bakhtin saw the mask as 'connected with the joy of change and reincarnation, with gay relativity and with the merry negation of uniformity and similarity.'

> It rejects conformity to oneself. The mask is related to transition, metamorphoses, the violation of natural boundaries, to mockery and familiar nicknames. It contains the playful element of life; it is based on a peculiar interrelation of reality and image.[12]

Isn't a peculiar interrelation of reality and image exactly the stuff of psychotherapy too?

The British director Peter Hall once asked actors who were preparing to use masks in his production of Aristophanes' comedy *Lystistrata* to choose from a variety of different ones set out on a table. They had slowly and carefully to put on their selected mask and confront themselves in a mirror. After a few seconds – no more – they had had to become what they saw, allowing the image to affect the way they talked, walked, thought and felt. There was only one proviso: if the mask felt untrue and provoked even a brief dishonesty, or if it was too alarming, the actor must immediately take it off and select another. 'Normally', says Hall, 'the image he sees liberates him; it can occasionally make him comprehend a whole new world.'

> By the use of the mask, the actor can change his age, his bearing, his physique – even his sexuality. He can express areas of his personality he did not know existed. But they are parts of him; otherwise he is pretending and being false.... The mask properly used does not obscure but reveals.

This does not happen immediately, any more than do the revelations of the consulting room. If the actor is being honest, said Hall, it may be weeks before he or she is able to speak through the mask the sentences that allow for improvisation rather than simply making guttural sounds and single words. But gradually, he 'becomes a person'.[13]

For some therapists, it may be axiomatic that through their relationships with their clients they too become more of a person, as they learn about themselves as well as the other; they may become more playful with the persona they bring to the consulting room as time goes on. Others may focus entirely on what their patients seem to be projecting on to them from key relationships in their early lives; they may continue to expect patients to be willing to relinquish their protective masks while keeping their own firmly in place. Others again may do a mixture of both, and the next chapter takes the debate into the consulting room. But before that threshold is crossed, just one more question.

What does it mean for people when they meet an unsmiling face and a humourless silence on the threshold of a new and unknown relationship, not just with another, but with themselves? As we've seen from individual accounts, this may be bewildering, often painful; it may increase feelings of uselessness and lack of worth. But more even than this, such an experience may already set expectations for the shape of the therapy to come. It may suggest that humour will have no place here, that there will be no wry smile at life's absurdities, no shared laughter to ease the hours. So already there may be an implicit warning: once across this threshold there will be rules about what is acceptable, all the more inhibiting because unstated. The consulting room may be anticipated as a place of dour and limiting ordeal rather than one which may offer lightness of heart and the chance to play with new possibilities as well as enduring experiences of anger, loss and grief.

This sort of expectation may suit some therapists well, because it accords with their theoretical beliefs. For others, the mockers on the way to Eleusis, and all those other jesters and buffoons whose antics parody the solemnities of religious ritual, may bring a dig in the professional ribs. The jokers may remind them that when the threshold is crossed between the everyday world and a sacred space, an over-rigid persona may inhibit rather than foster openness to aspects of psyche which are as yet mysteriously unknown. The antics at the bridge may suggest that if therapists can bring a little humour into the solemnities of their art, then perhaps their patients in turn will be encouraged to re-find enjoyment in a world that now may seem nothing but bleak.

Notes

1 Jacobson 114.
2 Lubell 33.
3 Taylor 89.
4 Ibid. 91–93.
5 Willeford 204–207; Sanders 200 *et seq.*; Hutton 96, 107.
6 Dinnage 61, 63 *et seq.*
7 Coltart, *Survive* 74–76.
8 Ibid. 75–76.
9 Knox 189–190.
10 Jung, 'Anima and Animus' 7:305.
11 Jung, *Dream Analysis* 74; 7:255.
12 Bakhtin 39–40.
13 Peter Hall, no page numbers.

Chapter 10

Power and promise

The mockers were not random in their targets. Through history, the people they jeered at were the ones who held the power: religious leaders, civic authorities and the wealthy. In their topsy-turvy world, power structures were crudely, bawdily, grossly reversed. Now let's hear it for the rest of us! From early times, here was also a rare chance for women to have their say. In ancient Athens, women gathered at the autumn festival of Thesmophoria to celebrate the goddess Demeter. Their husbands were obliged to allow them to attend, to defray all expenses – and keep out. For a day and a night, the women worshipped their goddess and did what women together still often do in many cultures: they bawdily, gleefully mocked their men folk and whooped up the age-old battle of the sexes. To this day, in the topsy-turvy of the Hindu spring festival of Holi, young men mock their elders and low caste women chase elderly Brahmins and pretend to beat them up.[1]

The topsy-turvy world doesn't just mock the structures of power in clear-cut Them and Us antagonism. It can also question accustomed social boundaries to intimate some other way for human beings to come together. At the midwinter Roman festival of Saturnalia, masters served a banquet to their slaves. This is often evoked as the original template for the Christmas-tide frolics of the Christian world, but it seems likely that the emphasis was more on equality than straight Them and Us reversal.[2] At another level, here's been an expression of solidarity among the underfolk. When 'Mere Folie' put on his glad-rags in fifteenth and sixteenth century Dijon, and travelled about town on her handsomely decorated cart with her bawdy, boozy entourage, today's pantomime Dames could well have jumped on board and felt at home. Mere Folie could deal out summary justice too – including to husbands who had beaten their wives during the Virgin Mary's month of May.[3]

Who will ever know whether those husbands went home feeling justified to beat their wives for the other 11 months? Those who see ritualised foolery as safeguarding social structures by a carefully contained release of discontent would probably think they did. Freud might have found his own views about regulating psychic energy within individuals somewhat analogous. In his analysis, relations with those who lay claim to authority and respect, and are in some sense 'sublime', demand a greater psychic expenditure than usual, in terms of self-restraint, speech and demeanour. If they can be 'degraded', then we can relax and the psychic energy saved can escape into laughter.[4] Today's stand-up comics might agree.

But as we've seen often enough by now, the forces of humour aren't easily regulated and contained. When Mere Folie's troupe attacked the local tax offices, the championing of the underfolk went beyond a joke. The cross-dressed English mummers who broke down unwelcoming doors to demand their due came only at Christmas-tide. But by the start of the nineteenth century, when 'General Ludd's wives' led crowds in the north of England to attack the new looms that threatened their livelihood, they brought a demand that wasn't so easily to be disregarded. The grievances of 'Rebecca' and the other cross-dressed protesters who led the mid-century Welsh riots against taxes were not jokes either. At one level, perhaps the cross-dressing was a device to evade detection. At another, perhaps it was an echo, however unstated, of a persistent and age-old topsy-turvydom in which the underfolk had their way.[5] And at another level again, here was a questioning of boundaries that reached right into the embodied sense of individual identity. Across place, time and culture, the topsy-turvy cross-dressing among both women and men goes beyond mockery: among priests and shamans from South America to Africa to Asia, it has intimated a sacred wholeness that contains and transcends even the most fundamental divisions, biological as well as social.

Psychotherapists hope that the people who seek them out will also learn how better to negotiate the boundaries between their personal forces of conscious control and the underfolk of the shadow; they may hope too that one day their patients become better able to intimate that mysterious dream of wholeness which lies beyond division. But therapists may also find it hard to remember just how powerful they can appear – and how inhibiting this may be to the work. Imbalance is built into the therapeutic relationship. People would hardly cross the consulting room threshold, after all, unless they hoped that here they would find some special knowledge and skills. Psychotherapists hope so too: that is what their often long and expensive training has been about. But consulting a therapist is not like consulting a lawyer or even a doctor. It is not generally to do with buying the skills that will sort out a relatively defined problem or symptom. In such consultations, even when their physical condition is most grave, people retain a sense of an essential, untouched 'self'. But often, when people come to a psychotherapist, they bring a dis-ease of their whole person, a loss of that very sense of self that enables them to make sure sense of their world. No wonder then that the therapist may be seen as offering a vital lifeline, even the promise of an ideal maternal care. Therapists may be imbued with everything that people feel that they themselves have lost – the ability to understand their condition, to evaluate it and to find an attitude that will heal, restore and even make them feel more whole than ever before. Psychotherapists know that part of their task is to accept these exaggerated, even magical views of their knowledge and skills, projected on to them as it were for safekeeping, until their patients are able, through the therapeutic work, to reclaim them for themselves.

Just how that is to be achieved, however, is at the heart of hot and sometime acrimonious debate, particularly at the analytic end of the art. The very word 'projection' has a dangerous edge: there's a force behind it which might not always be benign. Psychotherapists have become adept at ducking and diving with what's thrown at them, by categorising nuances of different sorts of projection and counter-projection, transference and counter-transference. But there is less agreement altogether about how to work with these.[6] For people on the receiving end, some of the techniques may seem to tip a proper use of knowledge and skill into a dangerous exercise of power. One woman had had at least six years of analysis before she decided that enough was enough. She'd still advise her best friend to seek therapy if she was in a terrible state; she'd even consider going back into therapy herself. But not into analysis.

> Avoid the claptrap, the power game, the sort of blank screen game. After all, you do have certain knowledge of yourself – obviously you don't have the same capacity to see yourself as the analyst does – but you do have a capacity to see yourself and they override it, they undermine it. My sense of myself is tremendously important to me, and if I'm enclosed somewhere with someone and no verification, then I'm at this person's mercy.[7]

The thread seems constant. Some 20 years later, this is how another woman remembered her own, very brief and 'totally and utterly useless' brush with analysis.

> The analyst didn't ever really say anything and I just didn't know what to talk about, what to do or what to say. I never even found out what it was that I was supposed to be doing.... I found his silence so punishing; he seemed to be completely in control.[8]

The two analysts involved might, of course, have a very different story to tell about these relationships. They might see in the perception of themselves as undermining, or punishing and controlling, a clear instance of transference on to them of crushing and damaging relationship patterns from the patient's past which need to be explored. But perhaps that would be just another undermining of the patient's here and now perception and experience – which is what they were complaining of in the first place. There's a sort of grim humour in this battle of perceptions, an echo of age-old debates about the ways in which people see and mis-see each other. As they say in the pantomimes: 'Oh yes I did!' – 'Oh no you didn't!' The comics can keep it up for minutes, and the audience joins in the chant, because somewhere, they recognise exactly what these protagonists are up against. In a consulting room replay, it's perhaps no wonder if patients sometimes end up scoffing at their therapists' interpretations; mockery, as we've seen, has ever been the weapon of the powerless against the powerful. (And let's not forget that patients may bring unconscious power issues of their own: in the shadow of the 'victim' lurks a tyrant.)

Back at the start of the twentieth century, the American psychologist William James was emphatic about the danger of interpretation. 'Thoughts connected as we feel them to be connected are what we mean by personal selves. The worst a psychology can do is to so interpret the nature of these selves as to rob them of their worth.'[9] Analytic theories and techniques may carry particular hazards, as the British Jungian analyst Robert Hobson eloquently explored all of 30 years ago. Therapists may, he says, suppose that by being opaque and faceless, they can produce 'pure transference'. But to the patient, such therapists may feel like 'unyielding stone', the very opposite of a partner in the two-person conversation which for him is what therapy is about. More malignly, this opacity may render the patient helpless. Lack of clarity about the structure of therapy, demands that seem for that person impossible ('Just say whatever comes into your head'), conflicting messages between a persona of studied neutrality and what the patient picks up of the therapist's unstated but actual feelings towards them: all these may contribute to a growing feeling of persecution. If in addition the therapist interprets everything the patient may say about them as manifestations of past relationships, says Hobson, they impede the patient's attempt to sort out what is illusory from what is part of the actual situation now. And this situation is bound to be influenced by the therapist's own characteristics, however consciously opaque they try to be.

> The patient is hindered in his efforts to discover his identity. Since all is illusion he can come to believe that all is distortion – his experience of himself and his perception of other people. Then all his emotional responses are 'neurotic'. There is no healthy bit left.[10]

The danger then, says Hobson, is that both parties get locked into a reciprocal 'persecutory spiral', caught in a mutual power-play in which each feels more and more impotent. The therapist tries to defend their method and their injured, if unconscious, omnipotence by an ever-greater rigidity in applying technique. The patient feels more and more helpless and driven to retaliate. At best, the spiral is broken if the patient manages to leave. Then the therapist may save face by calling them 'unanalysable' and finding a label for their 'sickness' which, says Hobson, can be roughly translated as 'it's all their fault'. But sometimes the patient, by now feeling weak, bad and resourceless in the face of a dominant and omniscient authority, can become trapped in a situation of extreme dependency, hostility and rage. The only way out, says Hobson, may seem to be suicide.[11]

Hobson may evoke the extreme; his own 'conversational model' of therapy brims with an empathy that's far from such grim therapeutic battles. But nearly 30 years on, many Freudian, Kleinian and Jungian analysts still believe that 'consistent interpretation of innate infantile fantasies' is what brings about psychological transformation. Jean Knox's recent list of ways in which this may be damaging echoes Hobson's – indication perhaps that not much has changed. People's attempts to create their own bridge of meaning from conscious to unconscious, she says, may be jeopardised if the therapist 'knows' their unconscious better than they do. If on top of that the therapist relies on a theory that sees unconscious intention as essentially negative, then the patient's sense of their own self and 'self-agency' may be damaged. And therapists may become locked in a constant internal power-struggle of their own – between the theory and technique they were taught and their intuitive sense of what actually works.[12] It's not hard to see from Knox's description how therapy might then become a malign version of Jung's 'two idiots in the same boat'. This may be especially so if the analyst's own power-battle between what they 'ought' to be doing and the urgings of the unconscious is a reflection of the dis-ease that brought the patient into therapy in the first place.

For Knox, perhaps the most potentially damaging aspect of an insistent therapeutic focus on 'innate infantile fantasies' is that it locks both parties into a relationship which is the very opposite of healing to the suffering mind. If the therapist understands everything that goes on as a replay of the patient's early days, then 'positive relational experiences' between them are dismissed as irrelevant or a sign of resistance to treatment. Yet these are the very experiences, Knox argues, for whose efficacy there is now neurobiological and other evidence.[13] (The next chapter explores this further.)

'Positive relational experiences' sound exactly what most people, psychotherapists or not, would dearly like to foster in their places of work and outside them, for their own sakes as well as other people's. So it may seem one of the odder aspects of the therapeutic art that so much in it seems potentially to stand in the way. Therapists are certainly aware of the dangers of power. As long ago as 1984, the psychoanalyst Charles Rycroft thought that many, as he himself, had gone beyond Freud's 'standard rules' of analytic technique to mitigate these. 'A surprising amount of the hostility and negative transference about which analysts write so much', he concluded, 'is, I believe, a response to authoritarian tendencies in either the therapist's personality or in the way in which he enforces arrangements which should be for the mutual benefit of both parties.' He himself believed that the practical arrangements of analysis should be arrived at by mutual agreement, and many other therapists, he thought, agreed.[14]

But there may also be something deeper going on here, less amenable to reason. In any relationship where one party is the (expert) helper and the other the (suffering) helped, power is there in the shadow, an inevitable part of the archetypal patterns at play in their relationship. In his classic analysis of *Power in the Helping Professions*, the Swiss Jungian analyst Adolf Guggenbuhl-Craig trenchantly considers the dual ancestry of the psychotherapist in medicine and the priesthood – and the unconscious shadow of these callings. Behind the doctor (and he himself was also a psychiatrist) he sees the charlatan, at best taken in by their own patter and nostrums, at blackest simply a cynical exploiter. Behind the clergyman stands the false prophet, the one who represses the inevitable uncertainties of belief to fall into a fundamental dishonesty or even a hypocritical exercise of spiritual power. For Guggenbuhl, these unconscious shadow figures are also psychotherapists' own, and if they take hold, the whole therapeutic endeavour is threatened by a dangerous psychological split. The therapist identifies with the archetypal figure of the healer, repressing awareness of their own psychological wounds; all their weakness is projected on to the patient, whose own capacities for health and self-healing are denied. The archetypal duality of 'healer–patient' which is the truth of both parties will continually try to reassert itself, but it can only do so, says Guggenbuhl, through a struggle for power. He is not optimistic that individual awareness can be of much help; he accepts Jung's gloomy dictum that greater consciousness inevitably constellates a darker shadow. His own best hope is both simple and demanding: a true openness to friendship and love that have nothing at all to do with consulting rooms or colleagues. Only in these other relationships, he thinks, will therapists find the authentic and necessary challenges to their shadowy urgings to power, dishonesty and hypocrisy, and so the potential for growth of their own deepest selves.

If there is humour in Guggenbuhl's diagnosis, it's fairly black and bleak. Yet maybe humour can also help unravel the entanglements of power in which psychotherapists and their patients can find themselves caught up. It has a good track record here. Roman conquerors knew the importance of humour to keep their sense of power proportionate. Their triumphal returns to their city were accompanied by clowns and satyrs, cavorting along with coarse obscenities, even screaming curses in their face. One of the clowns wore a golden crown and held another above the conqueror's head, constantly whispering in his ear 'Remember you are mortal.'[15] Medieval rulers also knew that they needed their court jesters, licensed to tell them what others did not dare to voice. 'Who is it that can tell me who I am?' asks King Lear as he begins to feel the terror of his inability to maintain his accustomed tyrannical power. 'Lear's shadow', answers his Fool, quick as a flash. Perhaps psychotherapists too could do with keeping their inner fool close in the consulting room, to remind them of their own power shadow and the inevitable limitations of their art. Perhaps it's when they don't take their theories quite so seriously that their patients will be better encouraged to take themselves and their own perceptions seriously enough. Together they may even be able to laugh at the power of negative patterns of relating – and by laughing, depotentiate them.

'Sometimes he laughed' recalls one of the people who visited the London existential therapist Anthony Stadlen.

> He laughed at my saying, for perhaps the twentieth time, that I suspected him of sleeping, or that I thought that he found his books hugely more interesting than my boring thoughts. Laughter in these circumstances might seem callous. In fact, it was always an instantaneous relief. His laughter somehow invited me to take a look, with him, at my ideas, helping me to see that they

were not based on reality. The laughter, somehow, was one of the ways that he treated me as an equal, not a lesser being; in that he was saying that we could laugh together. This had the effect of robbing these negative thoughts of their power, at least for that moment. Then he would help me work out where they came from.[16]

And then something else may be able to find its place: a shared therapeutic optimism that may be healing in itself. The mockeries and ruderies that have for so long and in so many places danced alongside the greatest and most solemn rituals of religion and state keep alive a hope and even a promise: things can be other than they are, and life can be better than it is today. Power will be less oppressive, and the law will bring true justice; ordinary folk will be not just heard but given their rightful, exuberant place alongside the great and the good and the men in suits. There will be not just enough for everyone to eat and drink, but a wonderfully delicious superfluity, enough to gorge and stuff and relish to the heart and stomach's content, with no dour heed to tomorrow's hangover to spoil the intense abandon to the life of the moment. Quite simply, life will be a lot more fun for everyone.

This is the egalitarian promise that underlies Mikhail Bakhtin's evocation of the enduring tradition of carnival, which for him finds its most glorious expression in the scatological excesses and adventures of Rabelais' gigantic monsters, *Gargantua and Pantagruel*. Here, where everything that belongs to the bodily 'lower stratum' is elevated above the spiritual and the aesthetic, Bakhtin finds a 'second world and a second life outside officialdom'. For him, this is a world in which 'no dogma, no authoritarianism, no narrow-minded seriousness can coexist, opposed to every ready-made solution in the sphere of thought and world outlook'. Carnival's grotesquely exaggerated celebration of the bodily has nothing to do with the individual carrier of the 'bourgeois ego'. For Bakhtin, this body is expression of the universal, unifying force of the people itself, insistently brought back down into the ever-fruitful womb of the earth to be continually regenerated and renewed.[17]

> The carnivalesque crowd is ... the people as a whole, but *organised in their own way,* the way of the people. It is outside of and contrary to all existing forms of the existing socio-economic and political organisation, which is suspended for the time of the festival.[18]

Bakhtin was writing in 1941, just a few years after the height of the Stalinist purges. He himself was continually and cruelly harassed by the regime for his writings and views; it was only in 1965 that his book was finally published. So it's not hard to see encoded, in his glorying of the Rabelaisian, a longing for another world to his own. In this world, Utopian egalitarian ideals would finally become enduringly embodied in the unquenchable regeneration of the whole people and celebration of the universal realities of the human body and spirit.

This Utopian longing is more than just a compensation for a harsh and punitive political regime. It is also a human yearning, kept alive by stories told across time and culture of a distant time when that ideal world already existed, and by the hope that what was once can come again. Once, so the stories tell, there was a time when humans lived in accord with divine order and in harmony with each other and creation itself. In ancient China, this was the state of Tao. This is what it was like during the Hindu Rama-raja, when the god-king Rama ruled his kingdom of Ayodya, and there was no need to impose morality through laws, because humans lived by his example. In the Golden Age of ancient Greece, men and gods lived in harmony in the bounty of nature. In the Judaeo-Christian tradition, this is what it was like in Eden, when God walked with Adam in the cool of the evening.

Of course these mythical states of divinely inspired natural order could not last. Eve must eat the apple of consciousness and their inbuilt urge for exploration must separate humans from that once-perfect unity with their gods. But the promise nevertheless remains encoded: things can be better than they are, and no aspect of human nature will bar us from participation. Humour's celebrations of everything that is most grossly, bodily, generatively human have always erupted around seasons of promise and hope – from the springtime promise of fertility and plenty to the darkest winter hope that spring will come again. The hope is there in the Indian spring festival of Holi just as it was in the ancient Roman Saturnalia, in the Christmas foretelling of a new order of peace and justice, and in Easter's promise that all may find their place within it.

Humour can help bring that transformative promise into life's here and now. The mockers on the road to Eleusis held the bridge between mundane realities and sacred space. The initiates returned to the world with the capacity to hold the experience of sacred mystery within their mundane selves. In a very different time and place, the Heyoka clowns of the Oglala Sioux turned everything upside down. They shivered in the heat and took their clothes off when it was cold. They spoke their words backwards and pretended to swim in dried-up river beds. When everybody laughed, it was not only for the moment. 'When the ceremony was over' said the holy man Black Elk,

> everybody felt a great deal better, for it had been a day of fun. They were better able now to see the greenness of the world, the wideness of the sacred day, the colours of the earth, and to set these in their minds.[19]

Today's psychotherapists may also find that tapping into 'lower levels' of consciousness brings a renewed vividness of life. They may recognise their own versions of a Golden Age in stories of ideal and blissful union between mother and baby – states from which the baby must as surely grow away as humankind must leave the divinely inspired order of those long-ago imagined times. What does therapy offer in return for that renunciation? Very many people come to the consulting room with a timid hope that they be acceptable in their humanness and not just as they 'ought' to be, that things will one day (and before too very long) be better than they are now, and that they will become more able to see 'the greenness of the world and the wideness of the sacred day'. One thing they will probably not want to find in the consulting room is full-blown, unbuttoned carnival. In that, they are unlikely to be disappointed.

But can they nevertheless hope to find a space for that spirit of laughter which, as Bakhtin saw it, 'frees human consciousness, thought and imagination for new potentialities'? Psychotherapy is devoted to trying to understand what must finally be beyond consciousness. But 'understanding', Jung once said, 'is a fearful binding power, at times a veritable murder of the soul.... The core of an individual is a mystery of life, which is snuffed out when it is "grasped".'[20] For both patients and therapists, humour may ease an opening to the mysteries that lie beyond theory and technique. The next chapter looks more closely at varieties of therapeutic relationship in search of how that might happen and what it might mean.

Notes

1 Nilsson, 104; Burkert 242–246; Apte 157.
2 Beard, 63 *et seq*.
3 Willeford 204 *et seq*.
4 Freud, 'Jokes' VIII:200–201.
5 Ackroyd 54.
6 See Wiener for a thorough exploration of the debate.
7 Dinnage 206.
8 Haynes 227.
9 James quoted in Hobson 202.
10 Ibid.
11 Ibid. 205–206.
12 Knox 188–199.
13 Ibid. ch. 9.
14 Rycroft 127.
15 Willeford 162.
16 Stadlen 5.
17 Bakhtin 39, 6, 3, 19.
18 Ibid. 255.
19 Black Elk quoted in Jacobson 194.
20 Bakhtin 49; Jung, *Letters 1* 31.

Chapter 11

Bridges and boundaries

Therapists' consulting rooms are full of bridges – between past, present and future, inside and outside, you and me. They are full of boundaries too – between past, present and future, inside and outside, you and me. Just how to negotiate the complexities of barrier and crossing is a question about the very nature of therapy; it fuels many tangled and even acrimonious theoretical and professional disputes. And as theory becomes practice and professional becomes personal, the question is found at the heart of some of therapy's most difficult moments as well – for both therapists and those who consult them.

Not much room for humour here, then?

But between bridges and boundaries is precisely where humour lives. It brings people together and cements bonds between them. It keeps people apart when they can't share the joke, and sets barriers between them with its cruelties and barbs. In the complexities of its actions is a bewilderment of opposites; humour drives us to analogy and metaphor in an attempt to grasp it and pin it down. Jung evoked the humorist Hermes-Mercurius, as ungraspable and uncontrollable as quicksilver – or as psyche itself. And for Jung, he could hardly be kept out of the consulting room, for he was the very spirit of therapy, both poison and panacea. Hermes is altogether at home in the hurly-burly marketplace of everyday life. But as messenger and guide between upper and lower worlds, he is also bridge-builder between conscious and unconscious, ego and Self. He is god of boundaries too: in the ancient world, the demarcation between inside and outside, your place and mine, was marked by his phallic stone herm. So he can keep the safe boundaries of the consulting room and the internal boundaries between ego and Self as well, guard against the psychological inflations that come when these are breached. But Hermes can as well lead astray, ignoring all boundaries with his thieving and mischief. So how humour is received in the consulting room seems rather important. If it isn't made welcome, then it's more than capable of sneaking its destructive energies into the unconscious shadows.

When Ann France began her second therapy with a few months of clowning about, it was with well worked out intent.

> I felt the need from the start to bring something of the more positive and lively me to the sessions. I felt that my previous therapist had got a false picture of me by hearing only about the gloomy side.... Only someone who knew what I could be like and feel like when happy could, it seemed, appreciate the sense of loss and desolation I had when depressed, because only then could they understand the gulf between the two ways of being. The sharing of jokes, taste for word-play and clowning about of those first few months were part of the wish to present myself as a whole person, lively and positive, as well as negative and depressed.... My playing around at the beginning of this therapy was largely inspired by the desire to bring a spirit of creative imagination to the exercise; not to take the rules of the game as immutable, but to redefine them, and see if a new construct could be obtained.[1]

How might such a plan be received? With an answering smile, a shared joke, a punning riposte? Or as a sign that something is going on unconsciously which is no laughing matter and cries out for interpretation? Maybe this person is not taking the therapy seriously enough. Everyone knows that children learn through play, but might we here do well to suspect a *manic defence*? The strategy might be an attempt at *manipulation*, an invitation to *collude*. It might be an act of *aggression*, a ploy to *control* the therapy and even *destroy* the therapist. And what if the therapist found something their patient said really funny? Would they keep a straight face, stifle their laugh in the interests of neutrality? If patients use humour as a defensive shield, therapists may use a defensive shield against humour too. What we find funny will certainly tell the other quite a lot about ourselves. So to muse about humour in the consulting room is also to muse about some of the most vexed therapeutic questions of all. How spontaneous and revealing of their 'real' selves should therapists be? And how revealing of their 'real selves' can people be if their therapists are not?

The conventions of therapeutic abstinence are the stuff of a thousand jokes; 'everyone knows' that analysts in particular expect their patients to reveal what is most hidden and painful while remaining resolutely mum about themselves. But for some people in the real world, the asymmetricality of the relationship may be painfully inhibiting. Here for instance is Alice, writing to her male therapist after a session:

> I felt obviously that I was opening myself up as much as possible, and had given all that I could of my feelings, my truth, but although we discussed them and I saw things in some ways in a different perspective it couldn't go deeper because it was a one-way thing. I don't want you to tell me all your feelings and thoughts of your own life but it is difficult when one feels one's giving like one's soul or Being and that it is one-sided. Although I felt you understood most of what I expressed, I wished perhaps you would reveal your true feelings and not act out the part of an analyst because I do feel at

times that when we are getting somewhere you say the right thing instead of what you really feel.²

And again, here's Carl talking to the woman he's been seeing for therapy for six years:

> What I fear are your private thoughts. You tell me it is all right for me to see or feel anything in this space, but what are you feeling? I don't care about your professional mask, your ethical responsibility. I am afraid that after all this time I am still not good enough, I just want to be a good boy. I want to be with you and I don't want all the formalities and artificialities of the setting. I think it's not an alright place and then sometimes you will tell me some small detail about your life; then you seem accessible and it changes everything.³

Both Alice and Carl seem to be saying something rather important here about therapeutic convention and how it affects them. Alice hints that the therapy might 'go deeper' if she felt that her therapist was more authentic, less of an actor playing a part. Carl finds that 'everything changes' when his therapist shows more of herself – and we can imagine that then he might become more of himself than a frightened boy.

In many therapeutic quarters, however, both Alice and Carl might seem to illustrate rather precisely the importance of therapeutic abstinence in evoking the transferential feelings that are the very fuel to analytic fire. In this view, the small self-revelation of Carl's analyst might even have turned down the heat and let him off the central task of fully understanding that fearful 'good boy'. Warren Colman, writing from the Jungian analytic end of things, finds the conventions of therapeutic abstinence so strong that they have become a super-ego injunction:

> [One] must always and only interpret the 'here and now' transference, maintain a neutral demeanour at all times, never make a personal disclosure, never acknowledge mistakes, never apologise, never answer questions and preferably don't ask them either, never say 'we', never accept presents, never look at photographs of the patient's family or read anything they bring into the room.⁴

Only joking? Some psychoanalysts of the strict observance might not see anything risible in Colman's satire. But here's something curious he discovered about these conventional wisdoms: the rationale behind them has hardly been explored. When he did a search on a specialist journal website, he found almost 600 references to 'interpretation' and nearly 1,000 to 'transference' – but only 50 or so to 'boundaries' or 'the frame'. He couldn't recall a single seminar on these during his own training, and they still didn't figure as specific topics on his society's training syllabus. It seemed to Colman that trainee therapists were expected to pick up the conventions as they went along, mostly through supervision and case discussions. For him, it was this lack of theoretical debate that contributed to the idea of 'good boundaries' becoming a super-ego injunction, a measure of the analyst's sense that they're 'doing it properly'. The injunction was certainly strong enough for Colman himself to feel a tension between what he'd been taught to do and what he actually did, and 'anguish' at the prospect of presenting his work to the prime carriers of what he took to be the professional super-ego, the British Psychoanalytical Society. In fact, his paper was not only warmly received but published in the *International Journal of Psychoanalysis*.[5]

So it doesn't do to judge people by the labels they wear or the institutes they belong to. But that doesn't make some central questions go away. What does happen – to both parties and the relationship between them – when therapists eschew any social conversation, or never let the mask of neutrality slip, or deflect every personal question with another about why it's been asked? What happens when the therapist resolutely privileges words over 'actions', and refuses, for instance, to look at someone's proffered family photograph, let alone accept a gift?

For some psychoanalysts such questions may crucially miss the point. Their concern is not with the therapeutic effect of their interventions. As expressed by the American Kleinian analyst Robert Caper in an instructive exchange with Colman, the task is solely to help patients to integrate repressed or split-off parts of their personality through steadfast interpretation of what's going on in the transference. And it is precisely the analyst's refusal to collude with the patient's unconscious expectations of him as 'external phantasy object' that makes the relationship 'real'.

> The patient may perversely idealise these collusions as ordinary sociability or friendliness, common human decency or warmth and empathy.... It is therefore quite important to keep in mind, when the patient feels that one is being 'real' and emphatic, that one may be unwittingly colluding with the patient's perverse attack on the analyst's and his own, reality sense.[6]

Compare and contrast:

> Unless patients can feel that they have reached their analysts, moved them, changed them, angered them, hurt them, healed them, known them in some profound way, they themselves may not be able to benefit from their analyses. From this perspective, psychoanalysis is a profound emotional encounter, an interpersonal engagement, an intersubjective dialogue, a relational integration, a meeting of minds.[7]

This is Lewis Aron, one of the architects of the 'relational analysis' which is already influential in North America and now infiltrating across the Atlantic. For these practitioners, there is no pre-existent world of the unconscious, whether in Jungian archetypes or Freudian understandings of personality, whether in people who consult therapists or in anyone else. For them, as Colman puts it, 'mind itself is social and ... the private subjective self, the intrapsychic "inner world", is subsequent to and contingent upon the relational context in which it is embedded'. Such a view makes a radical breach in 'traditional' assumptions: now the analyst can no longer be an impartial observer who 'knows' what is in the patient's unconscious. Interpretation becomes a matter of analyst and patient together making a meaning which in turn arises from the unique reality that the two of them have together constructed.[8] Interpretation is secondary, in short, to relationship, and as Aron's prescription dictates, the analyst had better be 'real' in it if it's to work. If someone brings a relational analyst a loaf of home-made bread they will probably not let it drop on the floor, as did one other because she knew it to be a 'manipulative seduction'. They will be more likely to accept it and think about its possible meanings with the person who brought it.[9]

In some quarters this approach may seem alarming indeed. 'Are waves of relational assumptions eroding traditional analysis?' asked one recent article from the British shore.[10] The very question conjures the threat of a watery tide of emotion eroding the firm contours of dry analytic land. There may even be a nasty undertow to these waves. If openness in the analytic relationship is what makes for 'real' therapy, are practitioners who rely on conventions of abstinence actually damaging those who consult them, by unintentionally replaying negative relational experiences from their past?

These 'new' questions are nearly as old as the troubled history of the talking cure itself; they can stir ancestral angers and disappointments to intensify today's debates. All of 80 years ago, Freud's disciple Sander Ferenczi was anathematised for both asking the questions and coming up with answers that today's relational practitioners would entirely recognise. In his last paper, he wrote of his most troubled patients, the ones who often fell into a 'trance' or state of dissociation, in which his interpretations were useless and only 'maternal friendliness' seemed to be of any help at all. What was going on here? Ferenczi concluded that these troubled people were unconsciously reliving a trauma of childhood sexual abuse which was not a fantasy, as orthodoxy would have it, but the very real and actual cause of such deep distress. And more: this painful reliving was actually caused by the 'professional hypocrisy' of the analytic relationship. He knew well and so did his colleagues, he said, that their professional masks of polite attention might be concealing very different emotions: they might be finding it hard to tolerate some aspect of their patients, or disturbed by what was going on between a patient and themselves. It was when he talked openly with his patients about his own reactions, Ferenczi found, that their deep distress was finally relieved. They became able to talk about the trauma of their past rather than so grievously re-enacting it. And why was this? Previously, in accordance with analytic convention, he had left 'something unsaid'; there had been something 'insincere' in the relationship which the patient nevertheless felt 'in all his being'. This concealment of what the patient already implicitly knew was essentially a replay of their original trauma. The analyst's 'honest openness' gave them a new and much-needed confidence in their own perceptions: what they already 'knew' was going on between them and the analyst actually was.[11]

Freud had already fallen out with Ferenczi about this sort of non-analytic behaviour, and about his 'maternal friendliness' which the gossip-mill well knew included both giving and allowing kisses. Why, Freud wondered, should independent thinkers about technique stop there? He saw the progression – first kissing, then pawing, then peeping and showing

> and soon we will have accepted into the technique of psychoanalysis the whole repertoire of demiviergerie and petting parties ... and Godfather Ferenczi, looking at the busy scenery that he has created, will possibly say to himself: Perhaps I should have stopped in my technique of maternal tenderness *before* the kiss.[12]

Beneath the concern for the hard-earned reputation of psychoanalysis, beneath the familiar mixture of anger and pain with which Freud so often met disagreement with his truths, there runs a question about the purpose of the therapeutic project which is still being asked. Freud thought that Ferenczi had become overwhelmed by 'the need to cure and to help'. This ran completely counter to his own unswerving motto: I dress the wound, God heals it. He himself could remember no childhood urge to help suffering humanity, only an 'overpowering need' to understand something of the riddles of the world; for him, the need to cure was a defence against unconscious sadism. Jung was another one who kept talking about cure and healing – and the echoes of *his* falling out with Freud still rumble in the analytic community today. Healing, or 'making more whole', was the very goal and process of Jung's project of individuation. But whatever Freud may have thought, Jung's motto was not, in fact, so very unlike his own. There was no room for analytic Godalmightyness in a process in which the ultimate healer was the Self and in which both therapist and patient were equally involved. For Jung, rather as for today's relational analysts, therapy was a dialectical procedure between two people, consisting in a comparison of their mutual findings; in this, the therapist must give up all pretension to superior knowledge to become 'a fellow participant in a process of individual development'.[13]

The continuing debates about the ends and means of therapy are perhaps inevitable, given the radical uncertainty of the project. People who read Ann France's story will know that her therapist did indeed often share the joke, and was nothing if not friendly and open in her response. In fact, says France, she became too nice. After an initial very positive year, they were both engulfed for two more by a horribly painful transference of love and hate, from which they were only rescued when another therapist intervened. This left France feeling that therapy was not for the vulnerable: 'a strong core of sanity is needed to survive it, or benefit significantly from it'. In the end, her own vulnerability overwhelmed her. At least one psychoanalyst, who was also the publisher of her book, has since asked whether her eventual suicide could have been averted had stronger therapeutic boundaries been maintained.[14] But an emphasis on the therapeutic relationship implies nothing about therapists being overly 'nice': an authentic anger may be as 'real' as anything else. Nor does a privileging of relationship over interpretation mean abandoning the proper security of therapeutic boundaries and frame. In fact, it may put a greater onus than ever on therapists to be aware, as Colman has underlined, that everything they say or do – or don't – is 'a real interaction that is having a real effect on the patient'.[15]

What lifts the old debates to a new level is that these days neuroscience can be called in aid. Therapists can learn from Jean Knox's *Self-Agency in Psychotherapy*, for instance, how the by now minutely observed interactions between mothers and their babies are for better or for worse encoded in the early maturing right brain hemisphere; they can follow her exploration of the lasting effects of these early mind–brain–body experiences on the growing individual's capacity to develop a reliable sense of a self who can have influence in the world. Ferenczi observed the damage done to his deeply traumatised patients by the therapist's professional mask. Knox could point him to a study which shows how distressed infants become after only three minutes of their mother showing them an expressionless face – and demonstrate how disastrous this sort of interaction may be to their developing sense of self if it persists to become a brain-encoded pattern. Ferenczi discovered that only 'maternal friendliness' seemed to help these patients. Knox could tell him how coercive left-brain to left-brain interpretation might seem to someone still relating at a developmentally earlier right-brain to right-brain level; she could suggest how he might map therapeutic responses which are empathically attuned to the individual's level of 'self-agency' and so enable further development. And these will be not just psychological healings but, thanks to its blessed plasticity, laid down in the very systems of the brain itself.

Here might seem cause for therapeutic optimism indeed, at last the promise for a reliable scientific base for theory and technique instead of the endless round of speculation and hypothesis. No wonder, perhaps, that Donald Kalsched reports from the United States that the 'new trauma paradigm' is becoming 'more and more "relational" and interpersonal, more and more informed by the findings of infant mother attachment studies, more and more interested in the early-forming infant brain, and especially in mind-brain-body integration'. These days, when the concept of 'trauma' is used to cover a spectrum of early developmental damage, the 'new paradigm' may seem widely relevant indeed. Kalsched sees these developments as essential to keeping therapeutic work both relevant and grounded. But he also emphasises that they are not in themselves enough: 'for *every self–other relational moment in psychotherapy there is also an inner event*, and I don't mean an inner event in the wiring or sculpting of the brain' (his italic). He means an inner event in the sculpting of the soul – in what

Jungians see as the relationship or axis between the ego and the Self. He and his patients know this because their dreams tell them so. And when they engage together with the mytho-poetic world from which dreams come, this is right-brain to right-brain communication too.[16]

Not many therapists, perhaps, will have the scientific education to evaluate how far their craft really is a matter of brain work. Many might wonder whether there are no inbuilt, genetically endowed qualities of mind and personality; they may feel that there is 'something beyond' a meaning that is created wholly through relational exchanges. But many therapists will also certainly know moments of 'real' relationship between themselves and those who consult them, and how movingly transformative these may be. Kalsched himself has given a telling experience of that.

He and Mrs Y had talked *about* the traumatic emotional deprivation of her early life. But they couldn't recover this *experientially*. Then one day she found some old home movies, taken at a family party. In them, she saw her two-year-old self, ignored as she ran crying from one pair of knees to the next until finally her nanny carried her off, kicking and screaming with grief and rage. She told Kalsched about this in her 'usual dispassionate way, covering her sadness with humour and sarcasm'. He suggested that they schedule a special session to watch the film together and so, after some laughing and joking to ease the mutual awkwardness of this departure from the analytic norm, they did. When they watched the party sequence for the second time, she broke down in tears, finally experiencing both grief for and empathy with her childhood self. Kalsched found that his eyes also filled with tears. He thought she didn't notice, but at the next session, this is what she said:

> You became a human being last time. I had neutralised you until you offered to see that movie with me and then I saw your tears. My first reaction was 'Oh God, I didn't mean to do that ... to upset you. Please, I'll never do it again....' But secretly I was pleased and deeply moved inside. You were so human. I couldn't get over it. I kept staying over and over, 'You affected him! You affected him. He cares about you!'.... It felt like the beginning of something new. All my armour fell away.

This was a turning point in the therapy. That same night, Mrs Y was visited again in her dream by a familiar and ominous male figure. But now, she and Kalsched could link the dream to the event, and understand more closely that inner figure which Kalsched influentially sees as both protector of the traumatised childhood self and jealous persecutor of any attempt to form trusting relationships.[17]

At least one commentator raised an analytic eyebrow to question Kalsched's abandonment of words for action when he arranged the film show; he wondered whether this wasn't a countertransference enactment containing elements of Mrs Y's psychopathology which needed working through. Kalsched's reply is instructive. He accepted that for most patients the therapeutic action of psychoanalysis had to do with interpretation. But he had not found that interpretation alone worked all that well with his severely traumatised patients.

> The analyst is dragged into the dance whether he likes it or not, and then the dance must be undone.... During this increasingly 'real' process, the original trauma is repeated with an object [i.e. himself] which neither exploits ... nor withdraws and retaliates. Slowly the traumatically compromised reality ego strengthens. Affects that were unbearable now get symbolic representation.[18]

Mrs Y and Kalsched worked together nearly 20 years ago, but they already knew the limits of interpretation alone and the value of the 'real' relationship. These days, Kalsched also emphasises 'the dance' in terms of right-brain to right-brain communication. But the right brain doesn't just give us the capacity for tears. It is the seat of humour and laughter too, and they're nothing if not 'real'. Might we at least wonder why they have only sneaked back into this chapter at the very last moment, and why they seem so hard to find in writings about the therapeutic relationship? But now let's give them a chance. The next chapter explores how therapeutic laughter may be when it's allowed to make itself comfortable on couch and chair – and what might be happening if it's not.

Notes

1 France 140, 141.
2 Hobson 210.
3 Haynes, 312.
4 Colman, 'Symbolic Objects' 193.
5 Ibid. 192–193.
6 Caper 345–346.
7 Aron quoted in Colman 'How I became a Relational Analyst' 473.
8 Ibid. 471–472.
9 The story of the dropped loaf comes from Knox 204; for a very different approach to proffered gifts see Colman, 'Symbolic Objects'.
10 Meredith-Owen.
11 Ferenczi.
12 Freud, *The Correspondence of Sigmund Freud and Sandor Ferenczi*, Letter 1216.
13 Freud, 'Sandor Ferenczi' XXII:229; 'Lay Analysis' XX:253; Jung 'Principles' 16:2, 7.
14 France 32; Young (no page given).
15 Colman, 'How I Became a Relational Analyst' 475.
16 Kalsched, *Trauma* 8–9, 117.
17 Kalsched, *Inner World* 20 es.
18 This exchange quoted in Colman, 'Symbolic Objects'194.

Chapter 12

No laughing matter?

Senses of humour are as slippery as mercury: what makes people laugh and why has kept philosophers puzzling for at least 2,000 years. But laughter itself is something different, less sophisticated altogether, and encoded, it's said, in the mammalian brain. Rats and chimpanzees don't make the chirrups and panting noises that humans call laughter in response to jokes – though it seems that chimps may learn to. They laugh when they're at play. Mammals laugh first and foremost, it seems, to form social bonds.[1]

Human animals are no different. When human babies first laugh at about three or four months old, it's the first sign that they are ready to engage with the world. And it's a two-way street: everyone knows just how joyfully engaging the laughter of small children can be to those around them. (In the Navajo tradition, there's a 'first-laugh' party to celebrate exactly that interaction.) Yet even attachment theorists, who have for so long and so carefully observed the minutiae of interactions between babies and their caregivers, have paid laughter little heed. John Bowlby, the first architect of their approach, gave it not one single mention in all his writings about the inborn behaviours that support the mother–infant bond; the nearest he got to it was 'babbling and smiling'. His successors have followed his lead. Judith Kay Nelson sought in vain for any reference to laughter in the voluminous literature on attachment; she found that it was simply assumed that the 'default attachment behaviour' of infants is crying.[2] It was only in 2012 that her own detailed study gave the laughter of infants and their caregivers its due – one more example, perhaps, of the persistent psychotherapeutic preference for unhappiness.

Nelson claims laughter as a key contributor to the interwoven neurobiological and bonding development on which the ability to regulate emotions and negotiate social relationships will rest. But the bias against laughter has echoed from the cot to the wider culture too. It wasn't until the end of the twentieth century that Robert Provine, professor of psychology and neuroscience at the University of Maryland, produced what he claimed to be the first empirical study of laughter's ways and meanings. Colleagues' reaction to his new interest was telling. Eyebrows were raised, he says: 'in the world of serious science, laughter is seen as a lightweight topic – an area lacking in clout and prestige'. But he himself thought that 2,000 years of pontificating by philosophers was enough: systematic observation of laughing people, and description of what they were doing, when they did it and what it meant, was 300 years overdue.[3]

Provine's first clues to laughter's essentially social nature came when he discovered that trying to measure it in the laboratory simply didn't work. When he showed his subjects an array of comedy shows, the most they offered in response, whether alone or in groups, was a few grudging chuckles. So he moved into the real world, and his findings are based on ten years of eavesdropping into when and how people actually laugh in everyday life. It doesn't do to stretch his findings, any more than he did himself. But we can perhaps mine them, together with other contributions, to play about with possible implications for laughter in therapeutic consulting rooms.

Here are some of the things that have been found about laughter's social nature and purpose. In ordinary life, rather than situations like comedy shows which are designed to elicit laughter, only between 10 and 20 per cent of laughter is in response to jokes. People laugh 30 times more in the company of others than they do on their own, and they do it a lot: the best estimate is no fewer than seven times in ten minutes.[4] And they do this first of all, it seems, for the same reason that chimps put on their 'play face' and make the panting noises that are their equivalent to laughing: to engage with others and show that they mean them no harm. People laugh at the end of sentences too, and not just because it's difficult to laugh and talk at the same time: they even do it, for instance, when they're signing rather than speaking. And, again, like chimps who laugh to signal that they want their play with another to continue, they do it because they want to maintain the contact.

These purposes of laughter do seem to be fundamental to being a mammal. After two years of watching rats at play, and listening in as they did it, the affective neuroscientist Jaak Panksepp concluded that the special chirruping that accompanied their games was indeed their equivalent of human laughter. And that's exactly how they chirruped too when Panksepp and his team tickled them. They even learned to recognise their own tickler, it seems, and chirruped as they chased their hand round the cage to get it to tickle them again.

So what happens to humans if the person on the receiving end doesn't respond to their laughing invitation to engage? It doesn't take a scientific study for any of us to recall the feelings of bewilderment, hurt and even shame that may flood in when our friendly overture is rebuffed. Such a response might seem insensitive and even unkind. It may also be quite unnatural. Everyone knows how contagious laughter is, and not only in the deliciously dangerous fits of the giggles that can explode when we catch another's eye just when we shouldn't. (Try taking a look at the video clip of Panksepp and his rat laughing as they play, and see if you laugh too.)[5] There's evidence now that this imitative response is encoded in the brain. Enthusiasm for patterns of mirror neurons in monkeys as the basis for human empathy seems to have become a bit dampened as research goes on.[6] But it really does seem that when someone laughs, the neuronal system that operates in their brain is mirrored in the brain of the other to cause the same action. (The same can be said for yawning, which as everyone knows is extraordinarily contagious too.)

Epidemics of laughter attest to the strength of this involuntary response, not just between individuals but in institutions and even entire communities. Provine finds it rather oversimplistic to pathologise these as outbursts of 'mass hysteria' or 'mania'. After all, as he says, it's often adaptive for social animals to coordinate their behaviour: when a mother becomes anxious in the presence of a stranger, so does her infant; when one animal in a group is spooked and runs, so does the rest of its group. 'At this level', he says, 'the group can be viewed as a superorganism, with each individual being a sensory and motor organ of the whole, contributing to the well-being of the group and sharing vicariously in the collective experience.'[7]

So when someone doesn't laugh back, can we wonder whether at the very least an opportunity for embodied connection and mutual well-being has been lost? We can wonder too, perhaps, about how safe the relationship will appear to the bond-seeking laugher. Professor Sophie Scott, from the Institute of Cognitive Neuroscience at University College London, points out that 'nervous laughter' ceases to be 'nervous' when the person on the receiving end laughs too. When this sort of laughter accompanies the imparting of difficult or even tragic news, it's often seen as unseemly, unsuitable or 'inappropriate'; to therapeutic ears, it might even signal 'repressed anger' or 'denial'. Scott, however, suggests that such laughter may be a plea to the other not to be upset, inviting a reciprocal laugh which reassures that together they will be able to manage this.

Might this have been at least something of what was going on in the encounter between the psychoanalyst Stephen Grosz and his patient Lily? She had returned from an extremely painful visit to her parents, and as she talked about it, he became aware of how each time he expected her to say that she'd been hurt or upset, she turned the tale into a series of 'comic bits'. At one point he 'stifled a laugh'; he mused to himself about the aggressive connotations of 'punch lines'. They agreed together that while the jokes diffused her great anger with her parents, they also took away any sense that she could challenge their behaviour without losing the last vestiges of relationship with them. As Lily said, 'It works, Mr Grosz, it works.' He wondered whether she might want him to laugh with her to show they were in agreement: they were the good guys, the parents the bad ones. 'My laughter absolved her of guilt – she didn't have to feel bad about making fun of her parents. She told me it was a relief when I laughed, and then she was silent. Neither of us spoke for some time.' But then Lily said that she'd been remembering her breakdown at boarding school, and her frantic phone call in the middle of the night, begging her parents to let her come home. They refused, and though things got worse and worse, she forced herself to stay. She went on:

But something had changed in me. My breakdown was like a furnace and what was burned away was any belief in my own feelings.... Even now it's very hard for me to trust my feelings. But when you laugh, it means that you believe my feelings, my reality. When you laugh, I know that you see things exactly the way I do – that you wouldn't have said no, you'd have let me come home.[8]

Reciprocal laughter builds connections of trust. By contrast, a lack of response to a laughing overture may reinforce distance and the barriers of social hierarchy. Provine was surprised to discover that speakers laugh more than their audiences – 46 per cent overall – but much more often when the speaker is a woman and the audience are men, and least of all when men are speaking to women. When it came to audience response, both women and men laughed more when the speaker was male than when they were female. This male superiority may start early. There's a study to show that when children are watching cartoons, girls laugh more often with boys than they do with girls, and reciprocate boys' laughter more than they do girls'. So laughter may be linked with social power structures. It may signal compliance, subordination or self-effacement, and be a way of ingratiating the laugher with the one with power. This seems as true in cocktail parties or schoolrooms as it is among, for instance, South Indian men who giggle in the presence of those of a higher caste, or the Bahastu of Central Africa who play the buffoon when they're with social superiors. When the one at the top doesn't share the laugh, social hierarchy is reinforced. In a study at a psychiatric hospital, for instance, the laughter was all top-down. Consultants made junior staff the butt of their humour, junior staff laughed at paramedics, themselves or patients – and none of them (in 'official' meetings at least) targeted anyone higher on the pecking order than themselves.

These research findings may offer further musings about humour and laughter in psychotherapy's shadowy power-plays. Therapists may indeed conceptualise their relationship with those who consult them as one of a mutual and egalitarian exploration. They may start from an assumption that neither of them can be privy to the truths of an unconscious that is greater than either of them, or an understanding that meaning is co-constructed rather than a given to which the therapist has the greater access. But even if this is all so, people still pay for psychotherapy because they trust their therapist's greater authority in matters of psyche. For all those who wish their therapist was more 'real', there may be as many who are glad they're not. And however 'real' the therapist, the proper rules and conventions of the therapeutic encounter and the essential asymmetricality of personal revelation ensure that inequalities can never be totally dissolved. Even the most benign 'developmental' theories and techniques also have their shadow side. Therapists who draw on ideas of 'the maternal' to conceptualise their role will be constantly aware that few people, for better or worse, have more power than a mother over her infant.

So a power-shadow seems to be inherent in the therapeutic relationship, and whether laughter is discouraged or welcomed in the consulting room may offer a clue to how it is worked with. Power wants to preserve its domain and keep people in their place; authority knows that its job is to establish and maintain a trustworthy environment in which people can learn to assume an authority of their own. Helping people to become *authors* of their own psychological story could be seen as a central therapeutic task. And one thing that can certainly be said about authority is that it's not afraid to enjoy a shared laugh. This, it knows, is one way of defusing the stultifying, growth-resistant hierarchies of power.

In *Trauma and the Soul*, Donald Kalsched writes about his six years of work with Mike, which stands out, he says, as helping to shape his own 'vocational destiny and self-understanding'. The rich nuances of his account would take us way beyond the scope of this book. But what does seem relevant here is the quality of mutuality that shines out from Kalsched's story, and the place of humour and laughter in building this. Mike's traumatic early parenting and particularly his suffering at the hands of an appallingly punitive father had led him to construct an angry, supermacho protective shell that went alongside a powerfully demonic inner protector–persecutor of his denied child-self. He found it extremely hard to expose any vulnerability, especially to another man. But from the start, reports Kalsched reports, they had a shared 'guy thing'. Both of them happened to be passionately involved in constructing their own homes and they would compare notes on their 'boy toys'.

> And of course his tractor was bigger than mine! He kidded me mercilessly about this and he loved the fact that I kidded him back! There was a lot of laughter between us and this helped in our developing rapport and trust.[9]

From the start, Mike taped his dreams and would play them back in the weekly sessions. Soon Kalsched noticed that the recorder was left running; intentionally or not, a good part of the session was being taped. They discussed this and Mike 'confessed': he liked to play the sessions back and think about what they'd discussed. This gave him 'more bang for his buck' as well. But, reports Kalsched, '[h]e especially loved our laughter together. The "music" of the session sometimes was as important as the content.' (Right-brain to right-brain communication rather than left to left?) Kalsched struggled with his own anxiety, vulnerability and feelings of exposure to allow this breach of the frame. 'It wasn't long' his next paragraph begins, 'before we discovered something of the early childhood vulnerability that Mike was carrying.'[10]

The work of inner integration and the gradual building of an sustaining axis between ego and Self was eventually reflected in Mike's growing ability to regulate his self-esteem, increasing tolerance of affect in relationships and an aliveness that Kalsched calls 'his embodied soul-full-ness'. About halfway through this process, Mike had a dream which made its own commentary on the sharing of authority between them.

You and I are sitting at a table and you're receiving a medical report on me – blood levels etc. [My wife] walks in. I say 'Don's got a great relationship with the dream-maker but his arms are too short to box with God.'[11]

The dream-maker has a sense of humour too.

Humour, laughter and 'kidding around' can create relationship. But they are born of it as well. It's not hard to imagine the potential for disaster in a super-imposed 'humour as technique', unrooted in relationship and unattuned to the relational moment. (Don't comedians know that if they get the timing wrong, it's not just the joke that 'dies' but they themselves?) As Provine found when he took recorded laughter from its natural living environment into the lab, it wasn't very difficult to analyse its stereotypical acoustic patterns. But the machine analysis would have been hard-pressed, he says, to analyse the subtle sonic distinctions between laughter that was sly, ironic or cheerful, sardonic or hearty. People in consulting rooms also need a relational context if they are to get the message encoded in each other's laughs.

In his work with Elva, Irvin Yalom knew something of laughter's different guises.[12] When she first arrived, he could find little to love in this dumpy, unattractive widow with her startling repertoire of facial grimaces. He amused himself by imagining introducing her to patients who had themselves developed facial contortions as a result of long-term tranquillisers. They would be instantly offended, he reckoned, because they would have thought she was mocking them. He almost laughed aloud. But he really disliked Elva too and her vicious rage that reminded him of his own mother's. He endured – and gradually, very slowly, began to warm to her.

And then: a turning point. Elva came in one day and plonked herself down in the chair with a 'Whew! I'm tired.' She had just played a round of golf with her young nephew and, in answer to Yalom's inquiry about how it went, she bent forward confidentially, and announced 'I whomped the shit out of him!' Somehow this struck Yalom as wonderfully funny. He laughed until his eyes filled with tears. Elva laughed too. She told him later that it was Herr Doctor Professor's first spontaneous act. The therapy was transformed; none of their hours together passed without a good laugh. He grew to appreciate Elva's qualities more and more, and her anger softened as she could talk about her sadness and loss.

But then her bag was stolen and all her trust in life was gone. Now finally she was forced to face the depth of her grief for her widowhood and the truth that she had no more special protection from ageing, loss and death than anyone else. Yalom had never seen her weep as she did now. He wondered what to do. But then he found an 'inspired gambit'. His eye lit on her huge bag, the very one that had been stolen (and eventually found empty and returned by the police). Wasn't she asking for trouble carrying around something that large, asked Yalom? Elva rallied: it was only medium-sized, she said, and besides, she needed everything in it. 'You've got to be joking!' said Yalom. 'Let's see!'

So together they hauled out everything in the bag and they inspected each item – from the 12 pens and three pencil stubs to the huge sheaf of photographs to the three bags of candies and plastic sack of old orange peels and the stapler. They laughed as they quarrelled over whether she really needed to carry each item. Finally the bag was empty and they stared in wonder at its contexts.

> She turned and smiled, and we looked tenderly at each other. It was an extraordinarily intimate moment. In a way no patient had ever done before, she showed me everything. And I had accepted everything and asked for even more.... That was a transforming hour. Our time of intimacy – call it love, call it love making – was redemptive. In that one hour Elva moved from a position of forsakenness to one of trust. She came alive and was persuaded, once more, of her capacity for intimacy.
>
> I think it was the best hour of therapy I ever gave.[13]

'The best thing a therapist can do for me', a man once told Peter Lomas, 'is to enjoy me.' What K, an experienced patient, wanted above all from a therapist was to be 'welcomed ... the kind of welcoming that has its roots in an utter, involuntary delight'. He was convinced that 'it is out of emotional engagement that mind comes', and he stressed the primacy of relationship – 'backed wherever possible and perhaps in defiance of the facts ... by an ongoing sense of "pleasure to see you"'.[14]

Laughter, as this chapter has outlined, is above all a reaching out for engagement – and the response it gets will shape the relationship to come. Human beings are complicated creatures; we know all sorts of ways of laughing back. These may range from a chuckle of recognition to barbed ridicule, from a wry acknowledgement of common human frailty to a mocking dismissal, and to every modulation in between. The laugher's invitation to engagement may find no answering laugh at all, nor even a smile. Some people, as we've seen, wouldn't dare to risk their dignity. For others, engagement may be psychologically impossible: people mired in the depth of depression find the laughter of others intolerable, a cruel marker of their isolation and grief. But at best, the invitation may find a wonderfully simple response: an involuntary meeting of laughter with laughter which comes *from somewhere else*. And then there is a moment of 'real' encounter between two human beings which is also, beyond all their separateness and difference, a meeting of Self with Self.

Notes

1 Unless otherwise indicated, information in this chapter from Provine, and Scott (personal communication).
2 Nelson 11, 2.
3 Provine 3–4.
4 Scott 27.
5 www.youtube.com/watch?v=j-admRGFVNM.

6 See Iacoboni for empathy and mirror neurons.
7 Provine 133.
8 Grosz 11–17.
9 Kalsched, *Trauma* 133.
10 Ibid. 134.
11 Ibid. 147.
12 Yalom, *Love's Executioner* 144–151.
13 Ibid. 151.
14 Lomas 33; K. 26, 28.

Chapter 13

Stories of life and death

So sacred were the Eleusinian Mysteries that none of the countless initiates ever revealed their secrets. But one story has persisted through the speculations of history: Iambe, now Baubo, was somewhere close to the heart of them. As the Church father Clement of Alexandria passed it on from an Orphic hymn, she was there at the very culmination of the ceremonies, not only reprising that gesture which had first roused Demeter from her deathly sorrow, but promising a future incarnation of Bacchus, god of ecstasy and dissolver of boundaries.

> She drew aside her robes, and showed
> A sight of shame; child Iacchus was there,
> And laughing, plunged his hands below her breasts,
> Then smiled the goddess, in her heart she smiled,
> And drank the draught from out the glancing cup.[1]

So this, said Clement, is what those famous Mysteries amounted to – the shameless worship of 'a poor grief-stricken woman and parts of the body which, from a sense of shame, are truly too sacred to speak of'. And there was more to incite his scorn. He had it on good authority that the sacred act of initiation consisted of no more than participation in and recounting of, a certain central ceremony: 'I have fasted, I have drunk the potion, I have taken [...] from the chest, and after acting, laid it in the basket, then taken it out of the basket and put it in the chest.' And what was this object too sacred to mention? Clement may not have known exactly, but he certainly knew he must 'strip bare their holy things and utter the unspeakable', and he gave his readers a long list of holy objects to suggest the sort of thing it might be: 'sesame cakes, pyramid and spherical cakes, cakes with many navels ... pomegranates, fig branches, fennel stalk, ivy leaves, round cakes and poppies'.[2]

Clement's Christianising purpose could hardly be more clear. But that hasn't stopped generations of scholars from puzzling over his words, and mining meanings of their own from this and other ancient hints and clues. Through all their delvings, Baubo has remained a constant – now lifting her skirts to make the goddess merry again, now companion to her daughter Persephone in her annual descent to the underworld and guide to her safe return. Baubo has even made her way to the very heart of the initiation rite: translated into a *baubo*, a modelled vulva, she is moved from chest to sacred basket to unite in sacred marriage with a *baubon*, a modelled penis, and thence returned to chest again.[3] Who will ever know? But through all the mystery – and perhaps because it remains so – what we can intimate is the *experience*. When one Antiphilus reported that his staff guided him to the temple uninitiated 'not only in the mysteries but in the sunlight', his blindness might as well have been psychological as physical.

> The goddesses initiated me into both, and on that night I knew that my eyes as well as my soul had been purged of night. I went back to Athens without a staff, proclaiming the holiness of the mysteries of Demeter more clearly with my eyes than with my tongue.

And here is Cicero, who thought these Mysteries were the best of all the excellent and indeed divine institutions that Athens had contributed to human life, instruments of civilisation itself. 'And as the rites are called "initiations", so in very truth we have learned from them the beginnings of life, and have gained the power not only to live happily, but also to die with a better hope.'[4] In the many human passages through life, death and rebirth, as the presence of Baubo at Eleusis hints, humour has a privileged place. It brings both the energy to endure and the fuel of transformation. This is told again and again, whether the story is about the small deaths of disappointment and its overcoming or survival through individual tragedies of trauma and loss; humour is their companion as people endure and surmount horrific tests of body and soul that only other humans know how to devise. When it seems that the situation could not be harsher, then humour will appear, as companion and guide back from the underworld. Shakespeare's Edgar, outcast and stripped of everything he held dear, finds words for this:

> The lowest and most dejected thing in fortune,
> Stands still in Esperance, lives not in fear:
> The lamentable change is from the best,
> The worst returns to laughter.
>
> *(Lear* IV, 1)

This is what comedians have always been up to: keeping that psychological truth alive, strengthening our courage through their reminders that tragedy and comedy are indissoluble partners. The monsters and devils who capered through medieval carnival took on the fear of what unimaginable fate might lie ahead; people never tired of laughing as they looked the mocked-up representations of hellfire in the eye. 'Here fear is destroyed at its very origin', says Bakhtin, 'and everything is turned to gaiety.' When Harlequin, that trickster clown, flew in his Mercurial sandals from Europe into early English pantomime, he promised that his audiences would see him 'dead and alive again' – and the sophistications of stagecraft gave him ever more elaborate representations of hell and heaven in which to work his transformations. To this day, stage magicians still replay his illusions and his message, as they saw their assistants in half and put them together again. Stand-up comedians still 'die' when the joke falls flat, just as actors 'corpse' when they get a fit of the giggles at precisely the wrong moment. These performers play out the human knife-edge between comedy and tragedy, and remind us of their bond. The comedian Jack Dee gave an example of that when he recalled a benefit evening on behalf of people with HIV-AIDS. It had been a great success, full of wonderful laughter. And then at the end, the mood completely changed. The organisers read out the names of all the people who'd died of AIDS-related diseases in the past year. There was total silence. And then people in the large audience began to shout out names of others they knew, and this went on for a full five minutes. 'I suddenly realised', said Dee, 'how many people there were in that audience who had brought their sadness with them. Through comedy, that sadness had been transformed into laughter.'[5]

We all know the knife-edge between comedy and tragedy. Don't we laugh till we cry and feel we could die of laughing? Humour may make it possible to live with sorrow; it challenges the tyranny of fear. But more than this: it takes on the fear of tyranny as well. Jung had little to say about humour in his published writings. But he was fond of quoting Schopenhauer's dictum: a sense of humour is the one truly divine attribute of human beings, the one which allows them to maintain their soul in freedom.[6] This may be as true in the inner world as it is in the outer. Humour challenges the tyrannical hold of negative internal judges and dissolves the fearful clinging to rigid assumptions. Its creative incongruities can keep open a window to other potential ways of being. And in times of greatest test, even where there is no external freedom at all, it is humour that may protect the freedom of the soul.

In *Nineteen Eighty-Four*, George Orwell's brilliantly chilling dystopia, Winston Smith mounts a timid rebellion against the tyrannical Party which dictates every aspect of its subjects' lives. His fearful hesitancy is constantly contrasted with his lover Julia's life-embracing fearlessness, her sexual passion, the sheer strength of her animal instinct. Winston rejoices in this; he knows it is the one force that could tear the all-powerful Party to pieces. But he cannot reach it for himself; he can only envy Julia when she tells him that her great difficulty during the mandatory daily ritual of the two-minute Hate is to keep from bursting into laughter. Under the terrible tortures ordered by O'Brien, his friend and protector so horribly revealed as his tormentor and inquisitor, Winston confesses, finally betraying Julia and so love itself. It is only in his last, broken hallucination that he can reach the point of laughter for himself. But by then, the laughter is all on the side of his tormentors and his laughter is also theirs.

> He was rolling down a mighty corridor, a kilometre wide, full of glorious golden light, roaring with laughter and shouting out confessions at the top of his voice.... With him were the guards and other questioners ... all rolling

down the corridor together and shouting with laughter.... Everything was alright, there was no more pain. The last detail of his life was laid bare, understood, forgiven.

Big Brother's world has won. O'Brien lays out its promise: 'There will be no love, except for the love of Big Brother. There will be no laughter, except the laugh of triumph over a defeated enemy.'[7]

In his gin-sodden afterlife, slumped in a cafe with his chessboard, Winston is visited by a sudden memory. He sees himself as a boy of nine or ten, sitting on the floor playing snakes and ladders with his mother; his little sister is there too, and all three are laughing as he excitedly shakes the dice for his throw. That was, he supposes, about a month before his mother disappeared. He pushes the picture out of his mind. It's only one of those false memories that trouble him from time to time. 'Some things had happened. Others had not happened.'[8]

In real life as well as fiction, laughter is the enemy of tyranny. At the beginning of 2015, a former employee of the 'Internet Research Centre', the Kremlin's on-line propaganda machine, broke ranks to tell of hundreds of workers engaged in posting at least 135 comments each day to bolster the official line. The constant creation of false criticisms of the regime and their 'loyal' refutation was, said Marat Burkhard, no laughing matter. 'You can get fired for laughing.'[9]

In Hitler's Germany, humour trod a knife-edge. As the regime tightened its grip and its ambitions, bolder challenges were increasingly suppressed; cabarets were closed and their performers persecuted. But the 'whispered jokes' continued. Did you hear the one about Hitler's visit to a lunatic asylum? When he enters, all the patients dutifully salute him. But one man's arm remains unraised, and Hitler furiously demands why. 'My Fuhrer, I'm an orderly, not a lunatic' comes the reply. As the war neared its end, the jokes became bolder. In one, Hitler is being driven through the countryside and his chauffeur accidentally runs over a chicken. Hitler says that he'll tell the farmer; he'll understand because, after all, this is his Fuhrer speaking. He comes back two minutes later, furious because all he got was a kick up the ass. Then they run over a pig, and this time the chauffeur volunteers to break the news. He staggers back after an hour, completely drunk and with a basket piled with sausages and other gifts. Hitler is astonished. He demands to know what the chauffeur said. 'Nothing special – just Heil Hitler and the swine is dead.'[10]

What else to do in the grip of the living reality – except laugh at the impossibility of laughter? After generations of practice, the Jews were the experts here; their jokes were always the edgiest. Five citizens of the Reich, goes one, were sitting in a railway waiting room. One sighs, another clasps his head in his hands, the third groans and the fourth sits with tears streaming down his face. 'Be careful, gentlemen', says the fifth. 'It's not wise to talk politics in public.' And one more. A man meets up with a friend. Nice to see you out, says the first. How was the concentration camp? Wonderful, says the second – breakfast in bed, then sport, then a three course lunch, then board games and a nap, then dinner and a movie. The first is amazed: 'The lies people spread! I was talking to Meyer and he told me nothing but horror stories!' 'And that' the second replies, 'is why he was sent back.'[11]

One of the very first books published in Germany after the war's end was a compilation of these 'whispered jokes'. Their historian Rudolf Herzog sees in this a reaching for exoneration, a turning to humour as a means of coping with the atrocities now revealed. And that, in his reading, was the story of the whispered jokes as well: they were a way of releasing pent up anger rather than an act of resistance. They targeted the foibles of individuals rather than the brutalities of the regime. They laughed at Goering's grandiosity, for instance, and the rows of medals on his chest ('to be continued on my back'). But they made no mention of the fact that he was a sadistic mass murderer. So the jokes were in the end useful to the regime: there was a note of fatalism in them that served it well. Even when people got too free with them, when they told too many and too often and were prosecuted for 'malicious attack' against the Reich, they were much more likely to be let off with a caution than to face time in jail. When persecution did become harsh, the jokes were likely to be a pretext; the regime had its eye on their tellers for other activities they judged more dangerous.

Herzog is far from the first, as we've seen, to understand humour as a way of letting off steam, adjusting the social pressure cooker to make conformity tolerable. This understanding of humour's purpose has stretched from medieval carnival to Freud and beyond, to the tradition of political jokes under the Soviet regime in Eastern Europe as well. Again, these target individuals rather than institutions, pulling the old ethnic storylines off the shelf to show just how stupid party leaders, apparatchiks and officialdom's heroes really are. Again, there's the note of fatalist acceptance. Isn't Russia proof that the Bible has it wrong when it says that first there's chaos, then order? Doesn't everyone know that first there's planning, then chaos? Why do Poles build meat shops two metres apart? So that the queues don't get mixed up, of course. And here's a question from Hungarians during the 1956 uprising. What's the difference between Nazis and Russians? Answer: for the Russians, everyone's a Jew.[12]

Does Comrade Stalin collect jokes? Yes, but first he collects the people who tell them. Not as often, however, as you might have thought: they and their jokes were tolerated, it seems, as one of his insurance policies. The persistence of the pressure cooker theory of humour may be persuasive; its victories can only ever be moral, not material. But psychologically, aren't moral victories the most important ones of all? Political jokes, we're told, arise in response less to brute force than to the special pain of spiritual violation, in situations where not just the body but the soul is under threat.

'Humour', says Victor Frankel in *Man's Search for Meaning*, his testimony to life that was born of the death-camps of Auschwitz,

> was [one] of the soul's weapons in the fight for self-preservation. It is well-known that humour, more than anything else in the human make-up, can

afford aloofness and an ability to rise above any situation, even if only for a few seconds.

And, he says, it's a capacity that can be cultivated in even the most crushing of human circumstances. 'The attempt to develop a sense of humour and to see things in a humorous light is some kind of trick learned while mastering the art of living.'[13]

Frankel knew well the cruelty of humour; it assaulted him as soon as he arrived at the camp. Experienced prisoners were amused, he recalls, when the naive newcomers, stripped naked and shivering as they waited to be herded into the shower-room, asked if they couldn't keep just their wedding ring, or a good-luck charm. Frankel himself furtively approached one of these old-timers to plead that he be allowed to keep the manuscript he'd rolled up in his jacket pocket, the fruit of his entire life's work. Did the man understand its vital importance?

Yes, he was beginning to understand. A grin spread slowly over his face, first piteous, then more amused, mocking, insulting, until he bellowed one word at me in answer to my question, a word that was ever-present in the vocabulary of the camp inmates: 'Shit'.

At that moment, says Frankel, the first phase of his psychological reaction to his incarceration was complete: 'I struck out my whole former life.'[14]

The mockery and insult of the weak by the stronger was ever-present in the life of the camps. But so was humour's moral retaliation against the brutalities of tyranny. 'Ordinary' prisoners mocked the privileged, envied Capos for their delusions of grandeur ('Imagine! I knew that man when he was only president of a large bank. Isn't it fortunate that he has risen so far in the world?'). Humour sneaked in through whatever cracks it found in the deathly days, and seized whatever chances it could. Frankel draws an analogy shocking in its associations: suffering is like the behaviour of gas, which if pumped in a certain quantity into an empty chamber will fill that space entirely, no matter the chamber's size. In the same way, he says, suffering completely fills the human soul and consciousness, whether it is great or small. From this absolute relativity of suffering's 'size' comes consolation: the smallest thing can bring the greatest of joys. He knew this when he was one of a transport of prisoners herded from Auschwitz, cramped in filth, in dread of the unknown destination. Eventually, after two days and three nights, they arrived exhausted at Dachau. No chimney, no crematorium, no gas! If anyone became too sick to work, they would have to wait until a so-called 'sick convoy' took them back to Auschwitz to die. 'This joyful surprise put us all in a good mood.... We laughed and cracked jokes in spite of, and during, all we had to go through in the next few hours.'[15]

The horrors of the Third Reich built inexorably over years. But when Brian Keenan arrived from his native Belfast to take up a university teaching post in

Beirut in 1985, he could hardly have predicted that months later he would be kidnapped by Islamic Jihad. He was held for over four years – for two months in isolation, and then together with the British journalist John McCarthy. They were shifted no fewer than 17 times, from tiny underground dungeon to freezing farmhouse and on, always blindfolded, never knowing what would come next. For three years, they were chained by wrist and ankle; sometimes they lived in total darkness. *An Evil Cradling*, Keenan's extraordinary account of the ordeal is, he says, an exploration of men 'in extremis', of the complexities of relationship between captor and captive – and of how men in the most inhuman of circumstances paradoxically grow and deepen in humanity. And from the start, humour was an indispensable companion and guide, both shield from and counterpart to the depravity and despair. In that underworld, humour threw open the doors to

> that vast playhouse of situations, resources and creative impulses that repulsed again and again the crucifying despair that drove some men to less than animal condition, to a state of inanimateness – day-long, unmoving silence when the body became, to all intents and purposes a corpse.[16]

Together, Keenan and McCarthy created the House of Fun – which was actually the name they gave to just one of their cells, but which might serve as well for what they made of them all. From the start, humour eased communication between these two very different men, unknown to each other and now enforced companions in the tiniest and most intimate of spaces. They horsed about until their laughter became uncontrollable, tinged with hysteria. Their stories became ever more ridiculous. They laughed when Keenan unwittingly scoffed a passion fruit full of maggots, and they laughed to overcome self-pity. They called up imaginary 'other people' to talk with and to make them laugh.

> In that laughter we discovered something of what life really is. We were convinced by the conditions we were kept in and the lives that we managed to lead that if there was a God that God was, above all else, a comedian. In humour, sometimes hysterical, sometimes calculated, often childish, life was returned to us.[17]

They celebrated that life, above all, in the competition of mutual insult, its unfettered scurrilities creating a gloriously imaginative counterpart to their fettered reality. 'We hurled this abuse with such pretended vehemence and at other times with such calm perverse eloquence that the force of it and the laughter pushed back the crushing agony of the tiny space.' In this, though Keenan doesn't say so, they fall into a long tradition. This is how people across time and space have negotiated intimacy and distance between themselves and another, and maybe managed pent-up aggression against oppressors too. From the ancient Norse and Anglo Saxon 'flyters' to experts in 'The Dozens' in contemporary Black

America (from fourteenth century English 'dozen' meaning to 'stun, stupefy or daze'), Keenan and McCarthy would have found companions in their sport.[18]

'You want anything?' a guard once asked them. Of course. They wanted many things they knew they wouldn't get – above all to know where they were and when 'this absurdity' was going to end. So yes, said Keenan, he wanted a colour TV, a bicycle and a grand piano. The guard was bewildered, so he repeated the request slowly, meticulously and with menace. The guards found such comic dismissal 'distasteful', says Keenan: '[h]umour was no part or condition of their lives'.[19] And in that, a central paradox: the captives, in the scope of their imagination, their endless inventiveness, the breadth of their memories, found Schopenhauer's freedom of soul, while the captors were chained by the unquestionable dogma and brutal dictates of their belief.

Humour is very far from being the only ingredient in such stories of life and death. These glimpses of people 'in extremis' have been chosen because they seem to speak so eloquently to the themes of this book. It doesn't do to exaggerate. Other people who have lived through similarly intense horror would tell other stories, in which humour may hardly feature at all. In Primo Levi's account of his own incarceration in Auschwitz, for instance, it is rarely glimpsed – and then almost always as a rictus of cruelty, mockery and insult. Such experiences may also seem too far from the safety of the consulting room for therapeutic relevance; it may seem almost an insult to those who have so suffered and endured to draw any analogy at all. The comparison is hardly of like with like: the purposes of totalitarian regimes are the polar opposite of therapeutic ones. In the first, the individual is no more than a disposable tool in the overall project; in the second the individual's well-being and development is the project itself. The first relies on coercion; the second is based in a negotiated contract which can be ended when the person paying for the service decides to go. What happens once the consulting room threshold is crossed may be uncertain, and such are the ways of psyche and life itself that truly no one may know what might happen next. But, with tragic exceptions, the same time, the same place, the same partnership, will reliably be there to honour the continuing search for meaning.

Yet there is no measuring one person's suffering against another's. As Frankel says, its 'size' is relative, and for the person immersed in it, it fills up the available emotional space. Consulting rooms are also places where stories are told of the soul's life and death, death and rebirth. This may be more than metaphorically so. The London relational psychotherapist Jane Haynes tells of a patient she calls 'Miss Suicide' ('SB') who by the time the two of them met, had already attempted suicide three times, and finally been dismissed by a psychiatric registrar as having a 'personality disorder' for which his services had nothing to offer. During her therapy with Haynes, SB made a fourth attempt to end her life. She bought whisky and paracetamol from Tesco, checked into a hotel and, to make very sure, put the supermarket bag over her head after she had taken the draught. And it was the bag that saved her, when the chambermaid looked in an hour later thinking the room was unoccupied. Through a combination of continued therapy and the skills of another, very different doctor, she slowly recovered her desire for life.

Two years after 'SB' had been discharged from any medical or therapeutic treatment, she was able to look back and laugh. She laughed when she remembered how she had botched a previous suicide attempt, she laughed as she remembered her growing impatience with conditions on the hospital ward and her fellow patients as she began to recover. She and Haynes laughed together over the sheer incongruity of a plastic Tesco bag being the instrument of her salvation: if she hadn't been wearing it on her head, the chambermaid would have thought she was just sleeping and closed the door. A lot of people, SB thought, would have been 'aghast' to hear so much laughter in a discussion of such times. But it's possible for the reader to hear in it a measurement of the distance between past despair and present life and a witness to her new perspective on herself and her sufferings. Perhaps it is also the sound of joyful celebration for a transformation of death into rebirth to life. And in that transformation, laughter had been a companion from the start. Recalling what it was that gave her courage when she first woke up in hospital, SB spoke of the positivity of the consultant and his optimism for her. 'Suddenly I didn't feel on my own ... and you having such a sense of humour; we laughed a lot together when you visited me while I was in the hospital.' Tragedy and Comedy, SB and Haynes agreed, are inlaid together.[20]

People who come to psychotherapy bring their own particular despair and grief for loss of life and potential, their own capacities for dealing with fear of the unknown and their own longings for the rebirth of energy and hope. They too may be imprisoned, in the deadliness of depression or in emotional experiences laid down in ever-present past trauma. They may be held captive by demonic internal figures as deceptively protective and malignly destructive as ever was O'Brien in *Nineteen Eighty-Four*. They may feel they exist in a living hell: indeed, Donald Kalsched, in *Trauma and the Soul*, takes Dante's account of Hell as metaphor for the present sufferings of encoded traumatic experience, and sees its monstrous cannibalistic ruler Dis as personification of psyche's dissociative defences.

People who come to consulting rooms, no less than anyone else, want to find or re-find what Frankel calls 'the art of living'. That art is humour's own. It can offer the step back from immersion in the psychological present which makes possible, however fleetingly, the beginning of self-reflection. It can defend against the mockery of inner tyrants and counter their crushing power with an assertion of the soul's inner freedom. It can bring perspective and free the imagination to glimpse the possibility of another, less constrained, way of seeing the world. And, importantly, these gifts can be cultivated. Frankel 'practically trained' a friend to develop a sense of humour through their agreement that every day each would concoct at least one amusing story about something that could only happen after their liberation. In solitary confinement at the start of his captivity, Brian Keenan made a deliberate choice about how to live with the 'delirium' in his mind. He would no longer try to stave it off, but let it take him where it would while he himself stood outside, watched and tried to understand. 'I would let myself go and watch myself, full of laughter, become the thing that my mind was forcing me to be.' It was, he says, a strategy he employed for the rest of his time in captivity.[21]

For Keenan and McCarthy, humour was soul-preserving. For at least one other of their occasional companions, it brought the rebirth of life from a living death. He lay still for days, says Keenan. The others felt anger and a fearful anxiety at the constant sight of this 'silent corpse'; nothing, it seemed, could arouse him from his torpor. Finally Keenan starts in on a hugely elaborate, hugely absurd story about the cheese factory he will launch when he's released. It will be entirely original, this cheese, made of pig's milk and of course mottled green because it's Irish. Now how, he muses, will he get that mottle into it? By now people are laughing and he becomes mock-indignant, spinning the story on. Even the 'dead man' begins to come to life. Then suddenly he says, very nonchalantly: 'You need to bury some copper wires in it Brian, and after a time pull the wires out...' 'Fuck me', says Keenan, 'how did you know that?'

> A man emerges back into life, not because of anything I have said, but the lunacy and laughter that is at the heart of our life beckon him back and he cannot resist it. There are many things a man can resist – pain, torture, loss of loved ones – but laughter ultimately he cannot resist.[22]

Notes

1 Clement 43.
2 Ibid. 43, 47, 45.
3 Lubell ch. 5.
4 Antiphilus and Cicero in Kerenyi 15, 193–194.
5 Bakhtin 39; Taylor 106–115; Dee in Cook 187.
6 von Franz 183.
7 Orwell 255, 280.
8 Ibid. 309.
9 Gallagher.
10 Herzog 40, 182–183.
11 Benton 34; Herzog 35.
12 Davies, 'Iron Cage' 25; Benton 48.
13 Frankel, 54, 55.
14 Ibid. 27.
15 Ibid. 72, 55.
16 Keenan xiv.
17 Ibid. 172.
18 Ibid. 127; Hyde 273–274.
19 Keenan 122, 123.
20 Haynes 238–259.
21 Keenan 78.
22 Ibid. 269.

Chapter 14

Looking back

When I mentioned to a young friend that I was thinking about writing this book, she paused. Then she said with great conviction 'There won't be any laughter in heaven.' I was startled and asked her why. 'There won't be any need for it', she replied. This exchange has stayed with me since, one more element in the puzzles and paradoxes of humour and its expressions.

Since then, I've learned that my friend's view has been shared by Christian theologians across the centuries. For them, so great is the inner joy in the state of perfection which is promised in Heaven that the consolations of humour are simply irrelevant. The Garden of Eden had already offered a foretaste of that harmonious bliss: indeed, as we've seen, the great abbess Hildegard of Bingen thought laughter no more than a proof of our fallen nature. It isn't only Christians who imagine these ideal states. The vision of a once-golden age seems universal across time and space, kept alive as a source of both hope and inspiration across countless generations. In a sense, Hildegard's idea is not so very far, theology apart, from Freud's view of childhood as that golden time when we had no need of humour to make us happy.

But that was then. Whatever we may believe lies ahead, it does seem that in the here and now, humour and the enjoyments it brings are one of this life's great blessings and consolations. This book grew out of a puzzlement: why, when this is something that 'everyone knows', does the art of psychotherapy seem to pay so little heed to it, in either theory or – as far as we're told – in practice? Not only that: in the extraordinary mixture of theory and subjectivity that makes a 'definitive' psychotherapy so impossible to achieve, there seem to be elements in both psychotherapeutic writings and the characteristics of some of its practitioners that far from encouraging humour are actually inimical to it. Why should that be? This exploration of the many facets of humour and its relevance to two people in a therapeutic consulting room began in an attempt to find answers for these questions. After all the excursions into where different people have found life's enjoyment and how they've explained this, it ends with me being more persuaded than when I set out of humour's psychological blessings, and more aware of what psychotherapeutic theory and practice may have been missing. As I hope has been clear, this is not to minimise the real sufferings that so often bring people to psychotherapy – or to gloss over the sufferings that humour itself may inflict. But it has been an attempt to explore an apparent imbalance in the way the psychotherapeutic arts have developed and to hold in mind that in life's dramas the masks of comedy and tragedy are ever intertwined.

One reason for a mistrust of humour, at least in psychological theories, may be a suspicion that it has to do with 'laughing it off', and avoiding painful truths that therapy is there to help people face. Therapeutic lore may not be short of negative interpretations here – 'denial', 'manic defence' and 'unconscious aggression' are three that come easily to mind. But these negative views seem in danger of disparaging humour's life-preserving consolations. There may be times when 'laughing it off' may, as the last chapter showed, be a vital defence: humour may be what makes endurable the threat of psychological or even actual death, and enables people to find strength defy it. The circumstances do not have to be outwardly extreme for this to be true. Humour can offer a new perspective to the bitterness of internal suffering, and bring a sudden enlivening sense that there could be something in the world beyond the imprisoning deadliness of despair.

Suspicion of humour also means that psychotherapeutic practice may deny itself opportunities to explore one of its own main purposes: helping people to find out more about themselves. 'Who am I?' is a fundamental question in many consulting rooms, and it runs through this book as well as one of humour's central preoccupations. Does my sense of myself come from within me or from the reactions of others? Why am I laughing at this person or that? Is it because I recognise, however ruefully and reluctantly, that somewhere we're alike – or because we just aren't? Already in Roman times, these were some of humour's preoccupations. Here's a joke from a bumper collection called *Philogelos*, or 'Laughter Lover'. A professorial type bumps into a friend and says in surprise 'I'd heard you'd died.' 'Well', says the friend, 'as you see, I'm alive.' 'But', says the prof, 'the person who told me was far more trustworthy than you are.'[1]

As we've seen, philosophers and others have tried over centuries before and since to pin down what humour is about. In tracing their theories and finding examples of what different people have found enlivening at different times, I've been struck by how little the basic triggers seem to alter. Human nature doesn't seem to change so very much. What does change over time, however, is what people are *supposed* to find funny. It's 250 years since Londoners were stopped from paying their penny to laugh at the antics of lunatics; today the sensitivity of the right-thinking consensus covers a good many more protected categories than that. But what people are supposed to feel and what they consciously or unconsciously do feel, are two very different things, as depth psychologists would be the first to point out. In the end, what makes people smile, or giggle, smirk or guffaw, is above all individual. That's why what constitutes humour is so impossible to pin down with certainty; my idea of its nature or yours is in the end as valid as Aristotle's or Freud's. But that's also why an individual's sense of humour is such a treasury of information about them – whichever consulting room chair they're sitting on. We may deplore the cruelties of humour, or jokes about people who are 'different' to an imagined norm, whether physically, intellectually or ethnically. But therapists will be more interested in working to find out what these are about than in banning them; they know the dangers of repressed and unacknowledged shadow selves.

So finding out more about our own sense of humour, and particularly its more shady aspects, can be a valuable signpost on the way to what Jung called 'individuation' – becoming more of who we individually are. Humour makes us more of ourselves, not just in terms of deeper self-knowledge, but also in our capacity to negotiate the world. Mockery, for instance, can be one of humour's cruellest weapons when directed against those we perceive as weaker than ourselves; we may have a lot to learn from this about our fear and denial of our own weakness. But mockery's purpose is also, as we've seen, the very opposite: it has always been the weapon of the weak against the abusively strong, one way of redressing the balance of power. This may be as true in the individual battle against tyrannical and disparaging internal voices as in dealing with the world outside. In such constant exchanges between individual and collective, humour can ease the negotiations, and bring us to together with others. Humour can help us out of the isolations of neurosis, the painful sense of alienation from other people; it can help us accept ourselves and others too.

Or it may do the very opposite. When we fail to get the joke, when we perceive others as somehow laughing at rather than with us, this may be wounding indeed. Humour is nothing if not two-faced; like alchemical Mercurius, who has darted in and out of these pages as one of the personifications of its spirit, it is both poison and panacea. This is reason enough, perhaps, for psychotherapists to be wary of 'using' it as a sort of technique; like stand-up comedians, they have to get the tone and timing right if the joke is not to 'die' – and they with it. Even then, they may be wrong-footed. There's a great deal in these pages about different ways in which people have 'used' humour. But at the same time and paradoxically, humour is essentially unbiddable, it doesn't know the meaning of 'appropriate'. It comes from *somewhere else* to catch us unawares and jolt us beyond what we thought we knew about ourselves and the world.

First comes the laughter, then the understanding of what it's about. The insight may be delightful; it may be embarrassing or even shameful. Humour doesn't care one way or another. It offers a different way of seeing, a moment of creativity and an invitation to imagine what would happen if things were like this instead of the familiar that. What we then do with the insight is up to us. One thing that has surprised me in the many theories and explorations of the uses and nature of humour is how little mention I've found of what I want to call its *innocence*. What we eventually make of what makes us laugh may be conditioned by all sorts of *oughts* and *shoulds*. But in itself, that humorous moment, that sudden laughter, is a flash of sheer delight, even of joy. Why else should the heart leap to hear the laughter of little children, when we and perhaps even they have no idea of what it's about? To laugh is to do ourselves a physiological good turn, as we've seen. But more than this: in that moment of delight there can be a profound psychological well-being. It may bring a precious and barely definable 'Aha!', a sense that now we re-cognise something we've always somewhere known. We may feel truly connected – not just to our own multiple selves or another person, but as part of that all-encompassing *something beyond* for which theologians, philosophers and psychologists have for so long struggled to find adequate words. In that creative moment, there is hope – that we may change, that life may be other than it seems. There is the possibility of laughter, however rueful, at our own folly which is also a sign of our common humanity. Then perhaps we can touch on an innocence which is not a naive nostalgia for pre-lapsarian bliss, but a good humoured acceptance of the human mixture of limitation and striving, light and shadow, as *just the way it is*. And then life's comedies and tragedies may come into a truer alignment.

For William Blake, the interweaving of the two was one of the *Auguries of Innocence*.

> Man was made for Joy & Woe
> And when this we rightly know
> Thro the World we safely go
> Joy & Woe are woven fine
> Clothing for the soul divine
> Under every grief and pine
> Runs a joy with silken twine[2]

What could be more therapeutic than an intimation of that silken lifeline? To set out to 'use' humour is bound to be a risky business, an opening to wounding misunderstandings as much as any hoped-for healing. To make humour a therapeutic 'project' is also to court the dangers of trying to constrain it to what is thought 'appropriate' or allowable. But to open the consulting room door more widely to whatever humour itself may bring, both its transformative possibilities and its potential risks, seems in itself a therapeutic act. Does it take anything more than a welcoming smile to make a start?

Notes

1 Beard 200.
2 www.poetryfoundation.org/poem/172906.

Bibliography

Editions cited are the ones I've used.

Freud's writings, unless shown otherwise, are in *The Standard Edition of the Complete Psychological Works of Sigmund Freud* (*SE*). Translated from the German under the general editorship of James Strachey, in collaboration with Anna Freud, assisted by Alix Strachey and Alan Tyson, and Angela Richards. London: Hogarth Press.

Jung's writings, unless shown otherwise, are in *The Collected Works of C.G. Jung* (*CW*). Eds Herbert Read, Michael Fordham and Gerhard Adler. Translated from the German by R.F.C. Hull. London: Routledge & Kegan Paul.

Ackroyd, Peter (1979) *Dressing Up, Transvestism and Drag: the history of an obsession.* London: Thames & Hudson.
Adams, Patch with Mylander, Maureen (1998) *Gesundheit!* Rochester, VT: Healing Arts Press.
Apte, Mahader (1985) *Humor and Laughter: an anthropological approach.* Ithaca, NY: Cornell University Press.
Aristotle (1915) *Poetics.* Trs. S.H. Butcher. classics.mit.edn/Aristotle/poetics.1.1.html.
Armstrong, Karen (2005) *A Short History of Myth.* Edinburgh: Canongate.
Aron, Lewis (1996) *A Meeting of Minds: mutuality in analysis.* New Jersey: Analytic Press.
Bader, Michael (1994) 'The Analyst's Use of Humor', in Herbert Strean (ed.) *The Use of Humor in Psychotherapy.* Northvale, NJ: Jason Aronson.
Bair, Deirdre (2003) *Jung: a biography.* Boston, MA: Little, Brown.
Bakhtin, Mikhail (1968) *Rabelais and his World.* Trs. Helene Iswolsky. Cambridge, MA: MIT Press.
Beard, Mary (2014) *Laughter in Ancient Rome: on joking, tickling and cracking up.* Berkeley, CA: University of California Press.
Beebe, John (1995) *Integrity in Depth.* New York: Fromm International.
Benton, George (1988) 'The Origins of the Political Joke', in Chris Powell and George Paton (eds) *Humour in Society: resistance and control.* Basingstoke: Macmillan.
Bollas, Christopher (1987) *The Shadow of the Object: psychoanalysis and the unthought known.* London: Free Association Books.
Bollas, Christopher (1989) *Forces of Destiny.* London: Free Association Books.
Bollas, Christopher (1995) *Cracking Up: the work of unconscious experience.* London: Routledge.

Bremmer, Jan (1997) 'Jokes, Jokers and Jokebooks in Ancient Greek Culture', in Jan Bremmer and Herman Roodenburg (eds) *A Cultural History of Humour: from antiquity to the present day*. Cambridge: Polity Press.
Bremmer, Jan and Roodenburg, Herman (eds) (1997) *A Cultural History of Humour: from antiquity to the present day*. Cambridge: Polity Press.
Brown, Peter (1991) *The Body and Society: men, women and sexual renunciation in early Christianity*. London: Faber & Faber.
Burkert, Walter (1987) *Greek Religion*. Trs. John Raffan. Oxford: Basil Blackwell.
Byatt, Antonia (2008) 'Introduction', in Harriet Harvey Wood and A.S. Byatt (eds) *Memory: an anthology*. London: Chatto & Windus.
Campbell, Joseph (ed.) (1955) *The Mysteries: papers from the Eranos yearbooks*. Trs. Ralph Mannheim. London: Routledge & Kegan Paul.
Caper, Robert (2003) 'Does Psychoanalysis Heal? A contribution to the theory of psychoanalytic technique', in Robert Withers (ed.) *Controversies in Analytical Psychology*. Hove: Brunner-Routledge.
Carey, John (ed.) (1999) *The Faber Book of Utopias*. London: Faber & Faber.
Chasseguet-Smirgel, Janine (1988) 'The Triumph of Humour', in Harold Blum, Yale Kramer, Arlene Richards and Arnold Richards (eds) *Fantasy, Myth and Reality: essays in honour of Jacob Arlow*. Madison, CT: International Universities Press.
Chesterfield, Lord (2012) *Letters to His Son*. Produced by David Widger. www.gutenberg.org/files/3361.
Clement of Alexandria (1960) 'The Exhortation to the Greeks', in *Clement of Alexandria*. Trs. G.W. Butterworth. Cambridge, MA: Harvard University Press.
Colman, Warren (2011) 'Symbolic Objects and the Analytic Frame', *Journal of Analytical Psychology* 56, 2, 184–202.
Colman, Warren (2013) 'Reflections on Knowledge and Experience', *Journal of Analytical Psychology* 58, 2, 200–218.
Colman, Warren (2013) 'Bringing it all Back Home: how I became a relational analyst', *Journal of Analytical Psychology* 58, 4, 470–490.
Coltart, Nina (1992) *Slouching Towards Bethlehem*. London: Free Association Books.
Coltart, Nina (1993) *How to Survive as a Psychotherapist*. London: Sheldon Press.
Coltart, Nina (1997) 'Nina Coltart', in Anthony Molino (ed.) *Freely Associated: encounters in psychoanalysis*. London: Free Association Books.
Cook, William (1994) *Ha Bloody Ha: comedians talking*. London: Fourth Estate.
Cousins, Norman (1979) *Anatomy of an Illness*. New York: W.W. Norton.
Critchley, Simon (2002) *On Humour*. London: Routledge.
Crowther, Catherine and Schmidt, Martin (2015) 'States of Grace: eureka moments and the recognition of the unthought known', *Journal of Analytical Psychology* 60, 1, 54–74.
Davies, Christie (1988) 'Jokes from the Iron Cage', in Chris Powell and George Paton (eds) *Humour in Society: resistance and control*. Basingstoke: Macmillan.
Davies, Christie (1990) *Ethnic Humour around the World*. Bloomington, IN: Indiana University Press.
Dickie, Simon (2011) *Cruelty and Laughter: forgotten comic literature and the unsentimental eighteenth century*. Chicago, IL: University of Chicago Press.
Dinnage, Rosemary (1988) *One to One: the experience of psychotherapy*. London: Viking.
Donleavy, Pamela and Shearer, Ann (2008) *From Ancient Myth to Modern Healing: Themis, goddess of heart-soul, justice and reconciliation*. London: Routledge.

Dundas, Alan and Hauschild, Thomas (1988) 'Auschwitz Jokes', in Chris Powell and George Paton (eds) *Humour in Society: resistance and control.* Basingstoke: Macmillan.
Eisold, Kenneth (1994) 'The Intolerance of Diversity in Psychoanalytic Institutes', *International Journal of Psychoanalysis* 75, 785–800.
Ferenczi, Sandor (1955) 'Confusion of Tongues between Adults and the Child', in Michael Balint (ed.) *Final Contributions to the Problems and Methods of Psychoanalysis.* Trs. Eric Mosbacher and others. London: Hogarth Press.
Fiedler, Leslie (1981) *Freaks: myths and images of the secret self.* Harmondsworth: Penguin Books.
Fierz, Henry (1982) 'Memory of C.G. Jung', in Ferne Jensen (ed.) *C.G. Jung, Emma Jung, Toni Wolff.* San Francisco, CA: Analytical Psychology Club.
Flowers, John and Frizler, Paul (2004) *Psychotherapists on Film.* Jefferson, NC: McFarland.
Fonagy, Peter (2003) 'Psychoanalysis Today', *World Psychiatry.* www.ncbi.nim.nih.gov/.
Forster, E.M. (1967) *Howards End.* Harmondsworth: Penguin Books.
Fotopoulou, Aikaterini, Pfaff, Donald and Conway, Martin (eds) (2012) *From the Couch to the Lab: trends in psychodynamic neuroscience.* Oxford: Oxford University Press.
France, Ann (1988) *Consuming Psychotherapy.* London: Free Association Books.
Frankel, Viktor (2004) *Man's Search for Meaning.* Trs. Ilse Lasch. London: Rider.
French, Nicci (2011) *Blue Monday* (and series). London: Penguin.
Freud, Clement (2001) *Freud Ego.* London: BBC Worldwide.
Freud, Martin (1957) *Glory Reflected.* London: Angus & Robertson.
Freud, Sigmund (1905) 'Fragment of an Analysis of a Case of Hysteria' *SE* VII.
Freud, Sigmund (1905) 'Freud's Psychoanalytic Procedure' *SE* VII.
Freud, Sigmund (1905) 'Jokes and Their Relation to the Unconscious' *SE* VIII.
Freud, Sigmund (1913) 'On Beginning the Treatment' *SE* XII.
Freud, Sigmund (1927) 'Postscript to the Question of Lay Analysis' *SE* XX.
Freud, Sigmund (1928) 'Humour' *SE* XX.
Freud, Sigmund (1930) 'Civilisation and its Discontents' *SE* XXI.
Freud, Sigmund (1933) 'Sandor Ferenczi' *SE* XXII.
Freud, Sigmund (1939) 'Analysis Terminable and Interminable' *SE* XXIII.
Freud, Sigmund (1985) *The Interpretation of Dreams.* Trs. James Strachey, ed. Angela Richards. Harmondsworth: Penguin Books.
Freud Sigmund (2000) *The Correspondence of Sigmund Freud and Sandor Ferenczi*, Vol. 3 1920–33. Ed. Ernst Falzeder and Eva Brabant, trs. Peter Hoffer. Cambridge, MA: Belknap Press of Harvard University Press.
Freud, Sigmund and Breuer, Josef (1991) *Studies on Hysteria*, Freud Penguin Library, Vol. 3. Trs. James and Alix Strachey. London: Penguin Books.
Gallagher, Paul (2015) 'Pro-Kremlin Troll Factory Where Every Day is Like 1984', *Independent*, 28 March, p. 25.
Goffe, Randy (2005) 'My Life as an Oompa', *Guardian*, 27 July.
Grosskurth, Phyllis (1985) *Melanie Klein.* London: Hodder & Stoughton.
Grosz, Stephen (2014) *The Examined Life.* London: Vintage.
Guggenbuhl-Craig, Adolf (1989) *Power in the Helping Professions.* Dallas, TX: Spring Publications.
Gutwirth, Marcel (1993) *Laughing Matter: An Essay on the Comic.* Ithaca, NY: Cornell University Press.

Hall, Edith (2006) *The Theatrical Cast of Athens*. Oxford: Oxford University Press.
Hall, Peter (1992) 'Behind the Mask', Programme note for *Lysistrata*, Old Vic, London.
Halperin, David, Winkler, John and Zeitlin, Froma (1990) (eds) *Before Sexuality: the construction of erotic experience in the ancient world*. Princeton, NJ: Princeton University Press.
Haynes, Jane (2009) *Who Is It That Can Tell Me Who I Am?* London: Constable.
H.D. (Hilda Doolittle) (1971) *Tribute to Freud*. Oxford: Carcanet Press.
Handel, Sydney (1988) *The Analytic Life*. Boston, MA: Sigo Press.
Herzog, Rudolf (2011) *Dead Funny: humor in Hitler's Germany*. Trs. Jefferson Chase. Brooklyn, NY: Melville House.
Hillman, James (1979) *Insearch: psychology and religion*. Dallas, TX: Spring Publications.
Hobbes, Thomas (2013) *Leviathan*. Produced by Edward White and David Widger. www.gutenberg.org/files/3207.
Hobbes, Thomas (2015) *The Elements of Law Natural and Politic*. www.Thomas_Hobbes.com/works/elements.
Hobson, Robert (1985) *Forms of Feeling: the heart of psychotherapy*. London: Tavistock Publications.
Homer (2003) *The Homeric Hymns*. Trs. Jules Cashford. London: Penguin.
Hustvedt, Siri (2009) *The Sorrows of an American*. London: Sceptre.
Hutton, Ronald (1996) *The Stations of the Sun*. Oxford: Oxford University Press.
Hyde, Lewis (2008) *Trickster Makes This World: mischief, myth and art*. Edinburgh: Canongate.
Iacoboni, Marco (2009) *Mirroring People: the science of empathy and how we connect with others*. New York: Picador.
Jacobson, Howard (1997) *Seriously Funny: from the ridiculous to the sublime*. London: Viking.
Jones, Ernest (1953–7) *Sigmund Freud: Life and Work*. London: Hogarth Press.
Jones, Kathleen (1972) *A History of the Mental Health Services*. London: Routledge & Kegan Paul.
Jung, C.G. (1934) 'Anima and Animus' *CW* 7.
Jung, C.G. (1935) 'Principles of Practical Psychotherapy' *CW* 16.
Jung, C.G. (1939) 'In Memory of Sigmund Freud' *CW* 15.
Jung, C.G. (1945) 'Medicine and Psychotherapy' *CW* 16.
Jung, C.G. (1946) 'Analytical Psychology and Education' *CW* 17.
Jung, C.G. (1950) 'The Syzygy: anima and animus' *CW* 9.ii.
Jung, C.G. (1951) 'The Psychology of the Child Archetype' *CW* 9.i.
Jung, C.G. (1951) 'Fundamental Questions of Psychotherapy' *CW* 16.
Jung, C.G. (1953) 'The Spirit Mercurius' *CW* 13.
Jung, C.G. (1954) 'Psychological Aspects of the Mother Archetype' *CW* 9i.
Jung, C.G. (1954) 'The Psychology of the Trickster Figure' *CW* 9i.
Jung, C.G. (1954) 'The Philosophical Tree' *CW* 13.
Jung, C.G. (1954) 'Archetypes of the Collective Unconscious' *CW* 9i.
Jung, C.G. (1973) *C.G. Jung Letters*. Vol. 1. Selected and edited by Gerhard Adler, trs. from German by R.F.C. Hull. London: Routledge & Kegan Paul.
Jung, C.G. (1984) *Dream Analysis*. Ed. William McGuire. London: Routledge & Kegan Paul.
Jung, C.G. (1995) *Memories, Dreams, Reflections*. London: Fontana Press.

K. (2008) 'Report from Borderland: an addendum to "what works?"', *Journal of Analytical Psychology* 53, 1, 19–30.
Kalsched, Donald (1996) *The Inner World of Trauma*. London: Routledge.
Kalsched, Donald (2013) *Trauma and the Soul*. Hove: Routledge.
Kerenyi, Karl (1967) *Eleusis: archetypal image of mother and daughter*. New York: Bollingen Foundation.
Keenan, Brian (1993) *An Evil Cradling*. London: Vintage.
Khaleelee, Olya (2008) 'Succession and Survival in Psychotherapy Organisations', *Journal of Analytical Psychology* 53, 633–652.
Knox, Jean (2011) *Self-Agency in Psychotherapy: attachment, autonomy and intimacy*. New York: W.W. Norton.
Kottler, Jeffrey (2010) *On Being a Therapist*, 4th edn. San Francisco, CA: Jossey-Bass.
Kubie, Lawrence (1994) 'The Destructive Potential of Humor in Psychotherapy' in Herbert Strean (ed.) *The Use of Humor in Psychotherapy*. Northvale, NJ: Jason Aronson.
Levi, Primo (1987) *If This is a Man and The Truce*. London: Abacus.
Lindner, Robert (1987) *The Fifty Minute Hour: a collection of true psychoanalytic tales*. London: Free Association Books.
Lomas, Peter (1999) *Doing Good? Psychotherapy out of its depth*. Oxford: Oxford University Press.
Lubell, Winifrid (1994) *The Metamorphosis of Baubo*. Nashville, TN: Vanderbilt University Press.
McDonald, Paul (2012) *The Philosophy of Humour*. Penrith: HumanitiesEbooks.
McGilchrist, Iain (2010) *The Master and His Emissary: the divided brain and the making of the western world*. New Haven, CT: Yale University Press.
McGuire, William and Hull, R.F.C. (eds) (1980) *C.G. Jung Speaking*. London: Picador.
Malcolm, Janet (1982) *Psychoanalysis: the impossible profession*. London: Picador.
Matter of Heart (1985) www.topdocumentaryfilms.com.
Meredith-Owen, William (2013) 'Are Waves of Relational Assumptions Eroding Traditional Analysis?', *Journal of Analytical Psychology* 58, 5, 593–614.
Midgley, Mary (1979) *Beast and Man*. Hassocks, Sussex: Harvester Press.
Molino, Anthony (ed.) (1997) *Freely Associated: encounters in psychoanalysis*. London: Free Association Books.
Moore, Thomas (1990) *Dark Eros: the imagination of sadism*. Dallas, TX: Spring Publications.
Nelson, Judith Kay (2012) *What Made Freud Laugh: an attachment perspective on laughter*. New York: Routledge.
Nilsson, Martin (1949) *A History of Greek Religion*. Trs. F.J. Fielden. Oxford: Oxford University Press.
Olender, Maurice (1990) 'Aspects of Baubo', in David Halperin, John Winkler and Froma Zeitlin (eds) *Before Sexuality: the construction of erotic experience in the ancient world*. Princeton, NJ: Princeton University Press.
Orwell, George (1955) *Nineteen Eighty-Four*. London: Secker & Warburg.
Otto, Walter (1939) 'The Meaning of the Eleusinian Mysteries', in Joseph Campbell (ed.) *The Mysteries: papers from the Eranos tearbooks*. Trs. Ralph Mannheim. London: Routledge & Kegan Paul.
Panksepp, Jaak and Biven, Evey (2012) 'A Meditation on the Affective Neuroscientific View of Human and Animalian MindBrains', in Aikaterini Fotopoulou, Donald Pfaff

and Martin Conway (eds) *From the Couch to the Lab: trends in psychodynamic neuroscience*. Oxford: Oxford University Press.
Perry, Philippa (2012) *How to Stay Sane*. London: Macmillan.
Phillips, Adam (1993) 'I Feel Guilty', in *London Review of Books* 15, 5, 11 March.
Phillips, Adam (1997) 'Adam Phillips', in Anthony Molino (ed.) *Freely Associated: encounters in psychoanalysis*. London: Free Association Books.
Phillips, Adam (2006) *Going Sane*. London: Penguin Books.
Pierce, Robert (1994) 'The Use and Abuse of Laughter in Psychotherapy', in Herbert Strean (ed.) *The Use of Humor in Psychotherapy*. Northvale, NJ: Jason Aronson.
Powell, Chris and Paton, George (eds) (1988) *Humour in Society: resistance and control*. Basingstoke: Macmillan.
Provine, Robert (2000) *Laughter: a scientific investigation*. London: Faber & Faber.
Radin, Paul (1955) *The Trickster: a study in American Indian mythology*. London: Routledge & Kegan Paul.
Rees, Dai and Rose, Steven (eds) (2004) *The New Brain Sciences: perils and prospects*. Cambridge: Cambridge University Press.
Rose, Steven (2004) 'Introduction', in Dai Rees and Steven Rose (eds) *The New Brain Sciences: perils and prospects*. Cambridge: Cambridge University Press.
Rycroft, Charles (1985) *Psychoanalysis and Beyond*. London: Chatto & Windus, Hogarth Press.
Sanders, Barry (1995) *Sudden Glory: laughter as subversive history*. Boston, MA: Beacon Press.
Scott, Sophie (2015) 'No Laughing Matter', *Biologist* 62, 1, 26–30.
Shepherd, Michael (1979) 'Psychoanalysis, Psychotherapy, and Health Services', in *British Medical Journal* 2, 6204, 1557–1559.
Singer, Thomas and Kimbles, Samuel (eds) (2004) *The Cultural Complex*. Hove: Brunner-Routledge.
Spiegelman, Marvin (ed.) (1988) *Jungian Analysts: their visions and vulnerabilities*. Phoenix, AZ: Falcon Press.
Stadlen, Anthony (2006) 'Why I Am Not a "Health Professional"', in *Hermeneutic Circular: Newsletter of the Society for Existential Analysis*, November.
Steiner, George (1961) *The Death of Tragedy*. London: Faber & Faber.
Strean, Herbert (ed.) (1994) *The Use of Humor in Psychotherapy*. Northvale, NJ: Jason Aronson.
Sultanoff, Steven (2013) 'Integrating Humour into Psychotherapy: research, theory, and the necessary conditions for the presence of therapeutic humour in helping relationships', *Humanistic Psychologist* 41, 4, 388–399.
Taylor, Rogan (1985) *The Death and Resurrection Show*. London: Anthony Blond.
Van der Post, Laurens (1983) *Jung and the Story of our Time*. London: Penguin Books.
Von Franz, Marie-Louise (1997) *Archetypal Patterns in Fairy Tales*. Toronto: Inner City Books.
Warner, Marina (1995) *From the Beast to the Blonde*. London: Vintage.
Wheelwright, Jane (1982) 'Jung', in Ferne Jensen (ed.) *C.G. Jung, Emma Jung, Toni Wolff*. San Francisco, CA: Analytical Psychology Club.
White, Jean (2006) *Generation: preoccupations and conflicts in contemporary psychoanalysis*. London: Routledge.
Wiener, Jan (2009) *The Therapeutic Relationship: transference, countertransference and the making of meaning*. College Station, TX: Texas A&M University Press.

Willeford, William (1969) *The Fool and his Sceptre: a study in clowns, jesters and their audiences.* London: Edward Arnold.
Withers, Robert (ed.) (2003) *Controversies in Analytical Psychology.* Hove: Brunner-Routledge.
Wood, Harriet Harvey and Byatt, A.S. (eds) (2008) *Memory: an anthology.* London: Chatto & Windus,
Yalom, Irvin (1991) *Love's Executioner.* London: Penguin Books.
Yalom, Irvin (1997) *Lying on the Couch.* New York: HarperCollins.
Yalom, Irvin (2002) *The Gift of Therapy.* London: Piatkus Books.
Young, Robert (2002) 'How Are We to Work with Conflict of Moral Standpoints in the Therapeutic Relationship?' Talk in CONFER series, *Power in the Clincal Relationship.* www.human-nature.com/freeassociations/young.html.
Young-Breuhl, Elisabeth (1988) *Anna Freud.* London: Macmillan.

Index

abstinence, therapeutic 42–3, 45, 100–1
Adams, Patch 62–3
agelasts 2, 66
alchemy 4–5, 8, 40
alliance, therapeutic 31
American Society of Neuroscience 77
Antiphilus 118
anxiety 31, 41
Archilous 81
Aristotle 52, 53, 61, 72
Aron, Lewis 102–3
Asclepius 40
Attachment theory 105, 109
Auguries of Innocence (Blake) 130

Bacchus 117
Bader, Michael 45
Bair, Deidre 22
Bakhtin, Mikhail 7, 87, 95, 97, 118
Barnam and Bailey Circus 57
Baubo (Iambe) 9, 12–13, 69–70, 117–18
Bedlam hospital 57
Beebe, John 44
Benedict, St 62
Bergson, Henri 52–3, 66
Bion, Wilfred 47
Blake, William 130
bodies 69–75
Bollas, Christopher 20, 26–7, 44, 52
Botticelli 74
boundaries, therapeutic 42–3, 99–107
Bowlby, John 23, 109
brain 75–8, 105–6, 107, 110–11
British Association for Behavioural Psychotherapy 35

British Journal of Psychotherapy 45
British Psychological Society 102
Burkhard, Marat 120

C.G. Jung Institute 24
Candid Camera (TV series) 63
Caper, Robert 102
carnival 7, 82, 87, 95, 118
Charlie and the Chocolate Factory (Dahl) 63
Charlie Hebdo murders 6–7
Chasseguet-Smirgel, Janine 20
childhood 54, 74, 82, 127
Chiron 40
Christianity 61–2, 73, 81–2, 127
Christmas-tide 81–2, 89, 90, 96
Chrystostom, St John 62
Cicero 51, 118
'civilisation' 75, 118
Clement of Alexandria 62, 117
clowns 71, 75, 81, 94, 96
Cognitive Behavioural Therapy 33
collective unconscious 25, 33, 75
Colman, Warren 45, 101–2, 103
Coltart, Nina 19, 30, 40, 42, 46, 84, 86
comedians 53–4, 66, 71, 114, 118, 119, 129
comedy 5, 53, 58, 85, 114–15; psychotherapy as 26–7
commedia del arte 53
concentration camps 120–22
Controversial Discussions 23–4, 25
couches, therapeutic 43, 44
court jesters 94
Cousins, Norman 63

140 Index

Critchley, Simon 52, 53, 55, 64
cross-dressing 90
Crowther, Catherine 54
cultural complex 33
Cyclops (Euripides) 74

Dahl, Roald 63
Davies, Christie 64–5
death camps 120–22
Dee, Jack 55, 66, 119
Demeter 9, 11–15, 69, 89, 117–18
depression 2, 31; of psychotherapists 41, 45
depth psychology 3, 20, 22–3, 25–6, 31, 32–3, 36, 73
Dictionnaire de l'Academie Française 56
Diderot, Denis 56
dissociation 77
Doolittle, Hilda 21
Dora 21
dreams 44, 51, 83, 106
Durer, Albrecht 74
dwarfs 55–6, 72

Ecclesiastes 62
ego 52, 54, 66, 99, 106
Eisold, Kenneth 34, 36
Eleusinian Mysteries 14, 70, 81, 83, 117–18
empathy 31, 110
enjoyment 3, 23, 41, 46, 47, 54, 113–15, 127
Enlightenment 56, 57
Eranos conferences 25
ethnic humour 63–5
Euripides 74
Evil Cradling, An (Keenan) 123

Face to Face (TV series) 22
Feast of Fools 82
Ferenczi, Sander 103–4, 105
fictional psychotherapists 39
Fleiss, Wilhelm 21
Flowers, John 39
Fonagy, Peter 33
Fordham, Michael 41–2
Forster, E.M. 73
Foster, Sir John 35
Fotopoulou, Aikaterini 77
France, Ann 99–100, 104–5
Frankel, Victor 121–2, 124, 125

Franz, Marie Louise von 21–2
freak shows 57–8, 63, 72
Freeman, John 22
Freud, Anna 23–4
Freud, Clement 21, 23
Freud, Sigmund 3, 5, 20, 21, 22–3, 34, 35–6, 43, 44, 51–2, 54, 66, 73, 89–90, 104, 127
Freudians 36, 92
Frizler, Paul 39

Garden of Eden 62, 96, 127
gelasts 2, 66
General Medical Council 35
Gift of Therapy, The (Yalom) 20
Goering, Hermann 121
Going Sane (Phillips) 19
Grosz, Stephen 111–12
Guggenbuhl-Craig, Adolf 93–4

Hall, Peter 87
Handel, Sidney 40
Harlequin 118–19
hatred 44, 45
Haynes, Jane 124–5
healing 3–4, 104
Henderson, Joe 25
Hermes/Mercury 8, 9, 99
Herzog, Rudolf 121
Heyoka clowns 96
Hildegard of Bingen 62, 127
Hillman, James 67
Hitler, Adolf 120
Hobbes, Thomas 52, 53, 61
Hobson, Robert 92
Holi 89, 96
hope 96
hostility 44, 51
How to Stay Sane (Perry) 19
How to Survive as a Psychotherapist (Coltart) 46
Howard's End (Forster) 73
humour: black 65–7; and bodies 69–75; cruelty of 55, 57, 63; and culture 5; curative effects of 31; ethnic 63–5; and human survival 20; and psychotherapists 1–2, 5, 19, 21–4, 29–32, 84; 'puerile' 7, 74–5; 'racist' 63–5; as social

regulator 71, 83, 89, 121; surprise and 53–4; theories of 52–3; *see also* enjoyment; jokes; laughter; mockery; smiles/smiling
humours (medieval) 4, 70–1

Iambe (Baubo) 9, 12–13, 69–70, 117–18
Impossible Profession, The (Malcolm) 24
incongruity theory of humour 52, 53
Independent School 31
individuation 44, 54, 72, 74, 104, 129
infant–mother relationship 105, 109, 112
inhibition 45, 54
International Journal of Psychoanalysis 45, 102
interpretation, therapeutic 92–3, 103, 107
Interpretation of Dreams, The (Freud) 21

Jacobi, Jolande 25
Jacobson, Howard 63, 64
James, William 92
Jesus Christ 40, 61
Jews 64, 65, 120–1
jokes 5, 6, 31–2, 51, 55, 57; political 121; about psychotherapists 39, 40; 'racist'/ethnic 63–5; whispered 120–1
Jokes and Their Relation to the Unconscious (Freud) 5
Journal of Analytical Psychology 45
Jung, C.G. 3, 4, 7, 8, 21–2, 24–6, 34–6, 42, 43–4, 54–5, 65, 70, 72, 74–5, 86, 93, 94, 99, 104, 119, 129
Jungians 36, 43, 44, 92

Kalsched, Donald 54, 73, 75, 77, 105–7, 113–4, 125
Keenan, Brian 122–4, 125–6
Khaleelee, Olya 36
Kimbles, Samuel 33
King Lear (Shakespeare) 118
Klein, Melanie 23–4
Kleinians 92
Knox, Jean 85, 93, 105
Kottler, Jeffrey 20, 33, 42
Kubie, Lawrence S. 29

laughter 4, 6, 29–30, 31, 41, 52–3, 54, 55, 56, 72, 94–5, 109–16; epidemics 111; nervous 111; and power 112–13; reciprocal 111–12
Lee, Stewart 66
Levi, Primo 124
Lewis, George 70
Lindner, Robert 3
Lomas, Peter 19, 34, 115
Love's Executioner (Yalom) 20
Lubell, Winifred 70
Luddites 90
Lying on the Couch (Yalom) 20

McCarthy, John 123–4, 126
McCormick, Elizabeth Wilde 2
McGilchrist, Iain 75–7, 78
Malcolm, Janet 24, 30, 36
manners, 'ordinary good' 84, 85
Man's Search for Meaning (Frankel) 121–2
Marceau, Marcel 86
masks 86–7, 105
Master and His Emissary, The (McGilchrist) 75
Mayo of Mexico 81
melancholy 446, 67
Memories, Dreams, Reflections (Jung) 22
Mercury/Hermes 8, 9, 99
Mere Folie 89, 90
Midgely, Mary 6
mirror neurons 110–11
mockery 81, 83, 87, 89, 91–2, 122, 129
monastic life 62
monkeys 72, 75
Moore, Thomas 66, 67
mother–infant relationship 105, 109, 112
movies, psychotherapists in 39
mythology 7–9, 69–70, 71, 117–18
myths 25–6

National Health Service 33
Navajo 109
Nazi Germany 120–122
Neil, A.S. 24
Nelson, Judith Kay 109
neuroscience 75, 77, 105
neurosis 43, 44, 86
neutrality, therapeutic 45, 85, 92, 101, 102

New York Center for Psychoanalytic Training and Research 30
Nineteen Eighty-Four (Orwell) 119–20

Oglala Sioux 96
On Humour (Critchley) 52
Orwell, George 119–20

Panksepp, Jaak 4, 110
pantomime 4, 53, 82, 89, 118
paradox 26
Paul the Apostle 61, 62
Perry, Philippa 19
Persephone 9, 12–15, 117–18
persona, therapeutic 86–8
Phillips, Adam 19, 31, 45
Philogelos 128
Plato 52, 61
pleasure 44, 46, 54
Poetics (Aristotle) 53
political correctness 64
political jokes 121
power 89–97, 112–13
Power in the Helping Professions (Guggenbuhl-Craig) 93–4
preconscious 25
priests 93–4
projection, psychological 87–8, 91; and counter-projection 91
Provine, Robert 109–10, 111, 112, 114
psychodynamic neuroscience 77
psychotherapists: as 'alienists' 40; and enjoyment 3, 23, 41, 46, 47, 54, 113–14, 127; and fees 41; in fiction 39; and humour 1–2, 5, 19, 21–4, 29–32, 84; in movies 39; preoccupations of 44–5; professional status of 34, 35; regulation of 35; suffering of 41, 42; training of 33, 35; unmet needs of 42
psychotherapy organisations 33, 36
Pueblo Indians 81
Punch and Judy 63

Rabelais and His World (Bakhtin) 87, 95
'racist' jokes 63–5
rage 44
Rebecca Riots 90
relational analysis 41, 102–3, 104

relief theory of humour 52
religious rituals and festivals 81–3, 88, 89, 96
repression 65
revelation of shadow 65
Ripley, Robert 57–8
Russia 120, 121
Rycroft, Charles 93

Saturnalia 89, 96
satyrs 74, 94
Schmidt, Martin 54
Schopenhauer, Arthur 21, 119, 124
Scott, Sophie 111
Self 55, 99, 106
self-agency 93, 105
sexuality 51
Shadenfroh 22
shadow, psychological 65–7
Shakespeare, William 118
shamans/shamanism 4, 40
Sheilagh-na-Gig 70
Singer, Thomas 33
smiles/smiling 20, 54, 84–5
social solidarity 64
solitariness 40
Soviet Union 121
Speigelman, Marvin 41, 42
Stadlen, Anthony 94–5
states of grace 54
Steiner, George 71
Strean, Herbert S. 29–30, 44–5
suffering of psychotherapists 41, 42
Sultanoff, Steven M. 30–1
superego, analytic 52, 66
superiority theory of humour 52–3, 55, 61, 63–4
Swift, Jonathan 56

Tertullian 55, 62
theology 61, 62, 127, 130
Thesmophoria 89
thresholds 81–8
tragedy 61, 87, 118–19
training, psychotherapy 34, 35
transference, psychological 43, 44, 45, 85, 91, 92; and counter-transference 91; negative 46

trauma 77, 103, 104, 105, 107, 113, 118, 125
Trauma and the Soul (Kalsched) 109, 121
Trickster 71, 72, 74–5, 78

unconscious 1, 2, 3, 7, 9, 26, 27, 32, 33, 35, 44, 51, 64, 65, 67, 83, 93, 99, 103, 112; collective 25, 33, 75; and ego 54
Use of Humor in Psychotherapy, The (Strean) 29–30

Van der Post, Laurens 22
virtues, therapeutic 31

Wheelwright, Jane 25
whispered jokes 120–1
White, Jean 31–2
Williams, Robin 63
Wizard of Oz (film) 56, 63
Wolff, Toni 22
Wounded Healer image 40, 41

Yalom, Irvin 20, 114–15

Zuni 81
Zurich Analytical Club 24, 25

Taylor & Francis eBooks

Helping you to choose the right eBooks for your Library

Add Routledge titles to your library's digital collection today. Taylor and Francis ebooks contains over 50,000 titles in the Humanities, Social Sciences, Behavioural Sciences, Built Environment and Law.

Choose from a range of subject packages or create your own!

Benefits for you
- Free MARC records
- COUNTER-compliant usage statistics
- Flexible purchase and pricing options
- All titles DRM-free.

Benefits for your user
- Off-site, anytime access via Athens or referring URL
- Print or copy pages or chapters
- Full content search
- Bookmark, highlight and annotate text
- Access to thousands of pages of quality research at the click of a button.

REQUEST YOUR FREE INSTITUTIONAL TRIAL TODAY — Free Trials Available. We offer free trials to qualifying academic, corporate and government customers.

eCollections – Choose from over 30 subject eCollections, including:

Archaeology	Language Learning
Architecture	Law
Asian Studies	Literature
Business & Management	Media & Communication
Classical Studies	Middle East Studies
Construction	Music
Creative & Media Arts	Philosophy
Criminology & Criminal Justice	Planning
Economics	Politics
Education	Psychology & Mental Health
Energy	Religion
Engineering	Security
English Language & Linguistics	Social Work
Environment & Sustainability	Sociology
Geography	Sport
Health Studies	Theatre & Performance
History	Tourism, Hospitality & Events

For more information, pricing enquiries or to order a free trial, please contact your local sales team:
www.tandfebooks.com/page/sales

Routledge — Taylor & Francis Group
The home of Routledge books

www.tandfebooks.com